STARS

in their

EYES

COLOR YOUR WAY THROUGH

HOLLYWOOD'S "GOLDEN" YEARS

by JANET W. LONG

THIS BOOK BELONGS TO

_____

Start_____ Finish _____

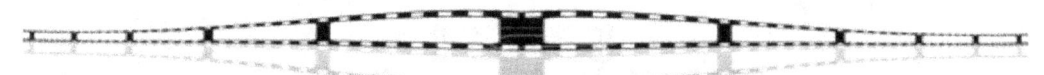

ETSY VINTAGE SHOP

"Go green! Buy vintage!"

https://www.etsy.com/il-en/shop/AdoptionsLtd

ETSY "JLA" SHOP

https://www.etsy.com/shop/JanetLongArts

[Photography & Watercolor prints & Hand Knits]

This book was developed by Janet W. Long in 2016.

I compiled these images, formatting them for your coloring pleasure.

ISBN-10: 1539941094
ISBN-13: 978-1539941095

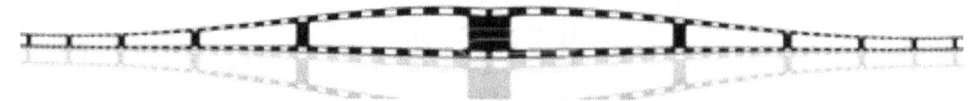

STARS in their EYES

Volume One

32 Vintage Grayscale Image for Your Coloring Pleasure.
Included here are actors, human & canine, born beginning in
1876. They are presented in chronological order.

THESE ARE ONE SIDED PAGES SO YOU DON'T HAVE TO CHOOSE WHICH PAGE TO COLOR!

INTRO...

I've chosen some vintage HOLLYWOOD images, pretty much family friendly, for your coloring pleasure! There's the glamor, child actors, some animals, pets of the stars & those who appeared in the movies we love. Let yourself relax & remember a simpler time portrayed by the, grayscale images in this coloring book.

I've developed these grayscale images for you with the tonal values in place. You add the color. Discover how your various pencils or crayons interact to create the colors you love.

You don't have to do the shading. It's already there. Just apply a layer of color & there's your picture! You'll find that even if you have only ONE red pencil, you can create many shades of red by using a blue, orange, purple underlay/overlay. Use as many layers as you wish. You're the colorist!

If you choose gel pens, felt tips, or other more 'liquid' mediums, please put a piece of cardstock or other paper behind your color work to catch any possible bleed through. You may want to cut out the pages to get a more open space to color. Go ahead, frame your work! Put it on your walls or give as a gift. It's ART!!

SOLI DEO GLORIA!

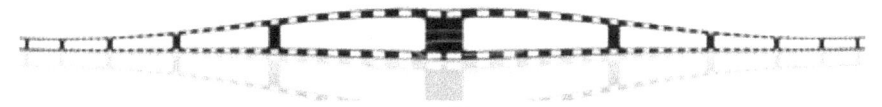

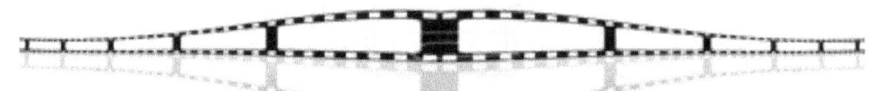

FEATURED ACTORS

1876-975 Madeleine Vionnet
1883-971 MAUDE FEALY
1886-964 LILY ELSI
1892-972 CLAIR WINDSOR
1893-993 LILIAN GISH
1904-986 CARY GRANT

1905-965 1920 CLARA BOW
1905-990 GRETA GARBO
1905-1993 MYRNA LOY
1934-ASTA FROM THIN MAN
w/ MYRNA LOY & WM POWELL
1907-1990 BARBARA STANWYCK

1921-2013 ESTHER WILLIAMS &
1920 – 2014 MICKEY ROONY
1921-2007 DEBORAH KERR
1920-1985 YUL BRENNER
1907-2003 KATHERINE HEPBURN
1908-1989 BETTE DAVIS

1908-1997 JIMMY STEWART & BEAU
1911-1989 LUCILLE BALL
1913-1967 Vivien Leigh
1915-1982 INGRID BERGMAN
1917-2012 CELESTE HOLM
1918-1987 RITA HAYWORTH & DOG
1922-1990 AVA GARDNER

1926-1962 MARILYN MONROE
1928-2014 SHIRLEY TEMPLE
1929-1982 GRACE KELLY
1931 Billie "BUCKWHEAT" Thomas "LITTLE RASCALS"
1938-1981 NATALIE WOOD

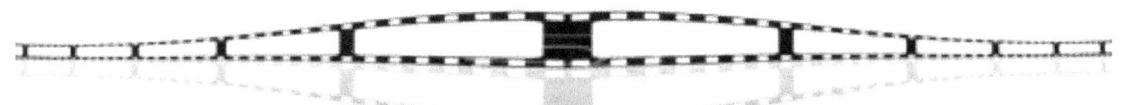

ACKNOWLEDGEMENTS

Thank you, Karen Thoden, for setting up a Facebook page
That facilitated my choice of images presented in this book. The
colorist listed below 'test colored' several of the
vintage Hollywood images for this book.

TRACE BROWN
LYNDA RODRIGUEZ
DENA MUELLER
ANGELIA MILLER
MICHELLE PILLON
PATTI HAVIAT
IRENE LAVERDIERE
THERESA HAMP KLEMAN
MAEVE THOMPSON
JENNY HUGHEY

YOU WILL SEE SOME OF THEIR ART ON THE BOOK COVERS.

A special "THANK YOU" to Dena Mueller, a kind, loyal supporter
has helped edit & grayscale some images
Dena participates in some worthy causes that might interest you:
Find them here: http://midsouth.wish.org/ & http://ucpark.org/

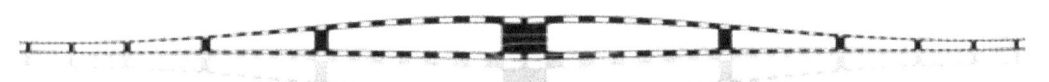

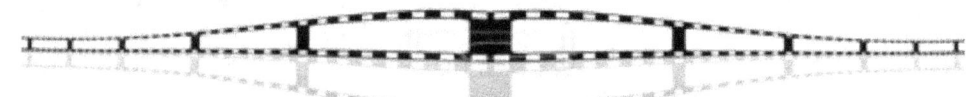

FIND ME:

AMAZON AUTHOR PAGE: ttp://amzn.to/2g7qeAZ

ETSY VINTAGE SHOP:
https://www.etsy.com/shop/AdoptionsLtd

ETSY SHOP, "JLA" :
https://www.janetlongarts/shop/Etsy.com

ETSY "JLA" RETAIL SHOP ON FACEBOOK:
https://www.facebook.com/Janet-Long-Arts-192517394097105/

ETSY VINTAGE RETAIL SHOP on FACEBOOK:
http://bit.ly/2e33zFD

TWITTER: https://twitter.com/jan43q
PINTEREST: http://pinterest.com/janetlongarts/
LINKEDIN: ttp://www.linkedin.com/profile/view?...

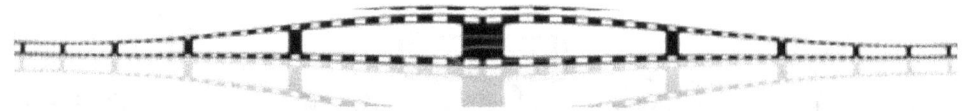

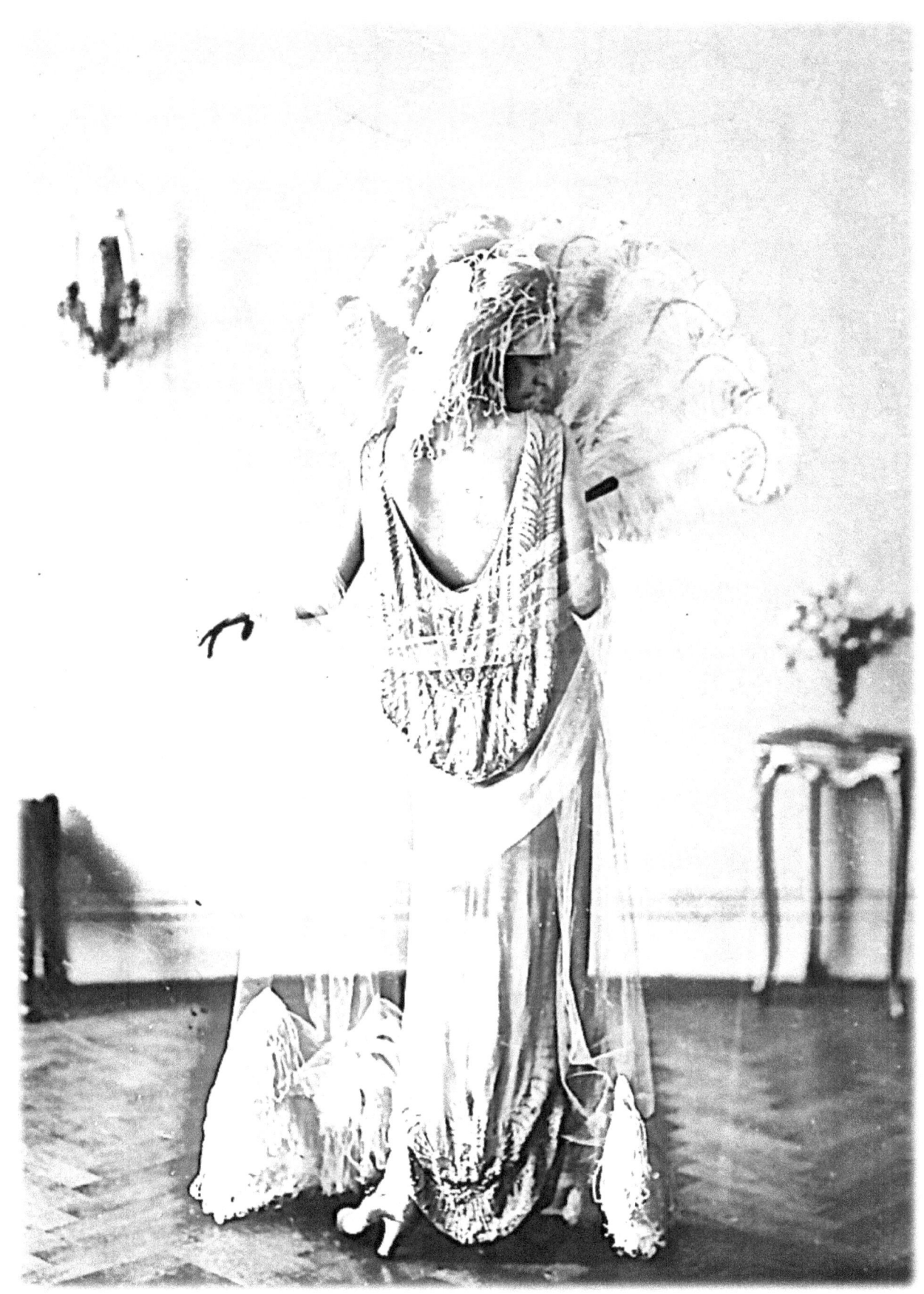

MADELEINE VIONNET

MADELEINE VIONNET 1876-1975
in a Norman Hartnell dress, c. 1920s
AMAZON AUTHOR PAGE: http://amzn.to/2g7qeAZ

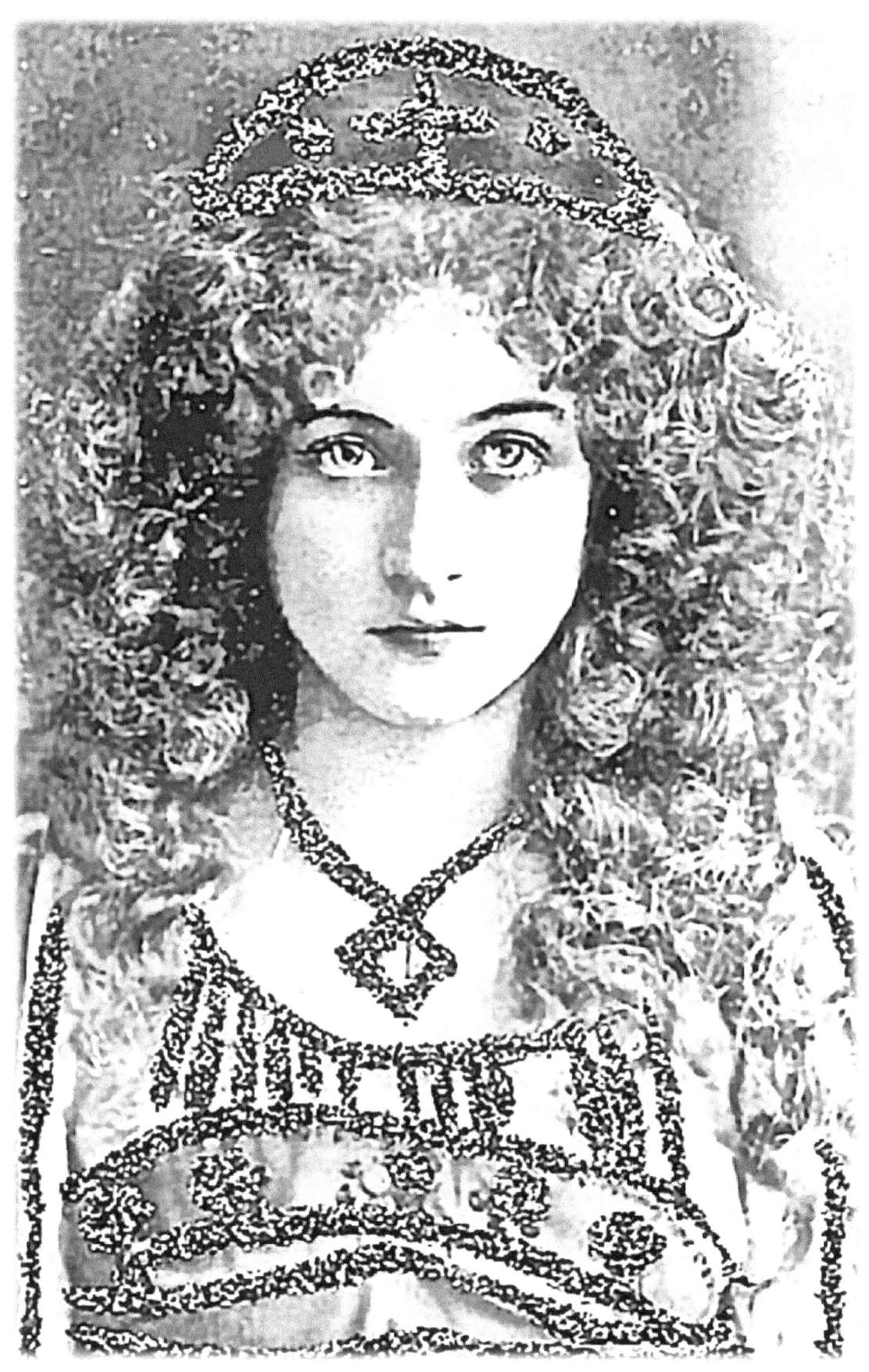

MISS MAUDE FEALY

MAUDE FEALY 1883-1971

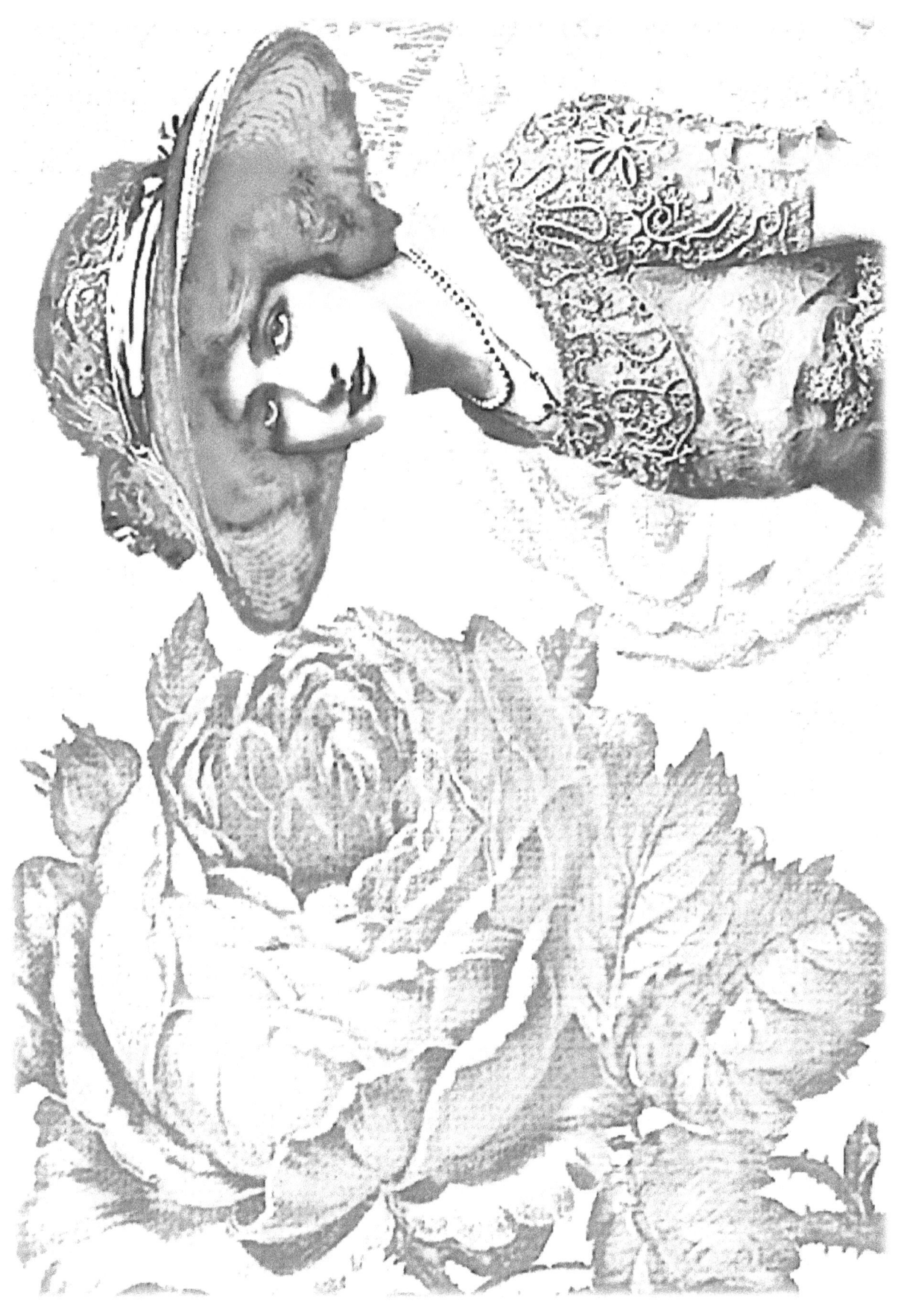

LILY ELSIE

LILY ELSIE 1886-1964 Actress & Singer
AMAZON AUTHOR PAGE: http://amzn.to/2g7qeAZ

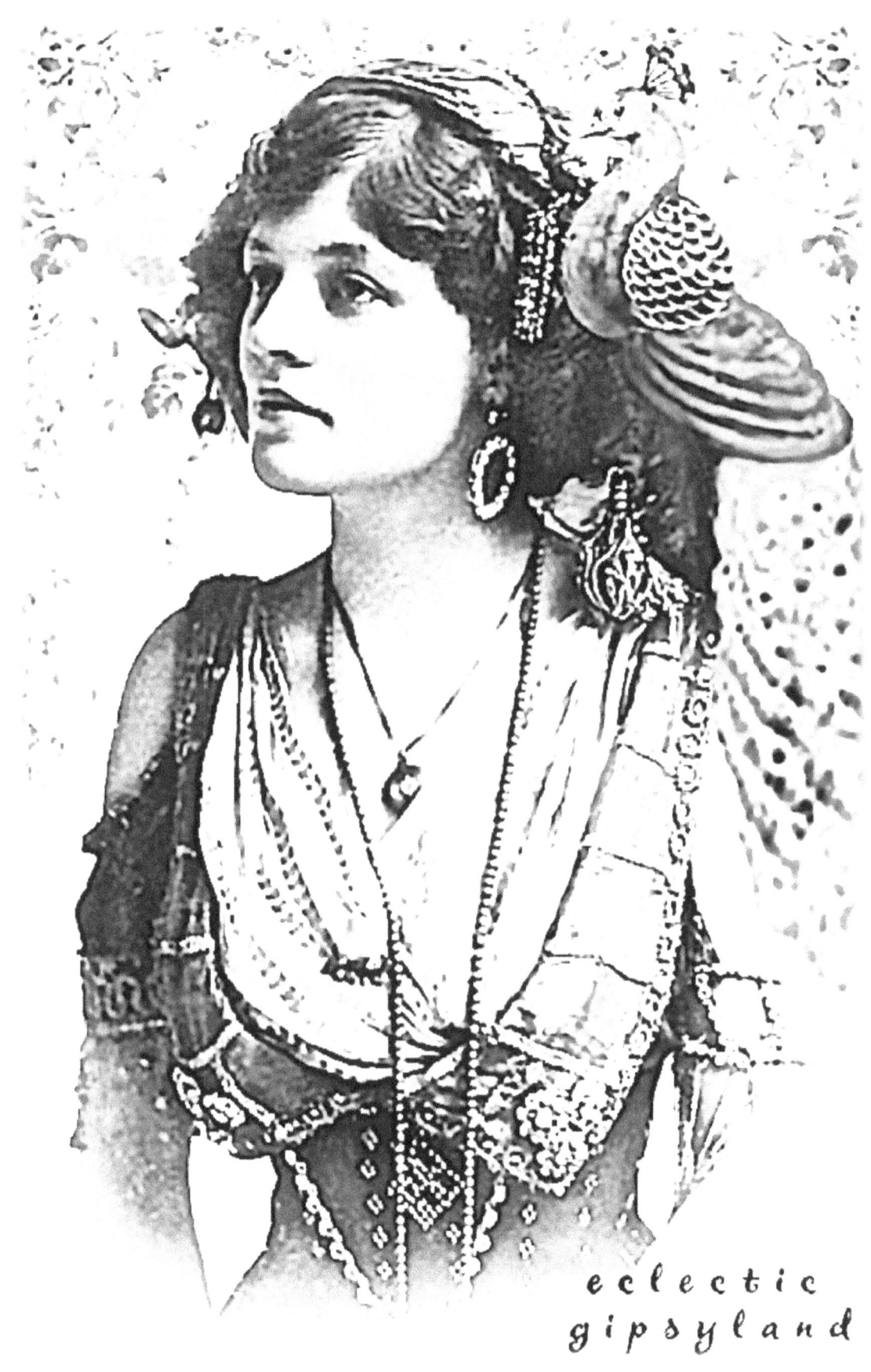

eclectic gipsyland

LILY ELSIE

LILY ELSIE 1886-1964 "Beautiful Gypsy"
AMAZON AUTHOR PAGE: http://amzn.to/2g7qeAZ

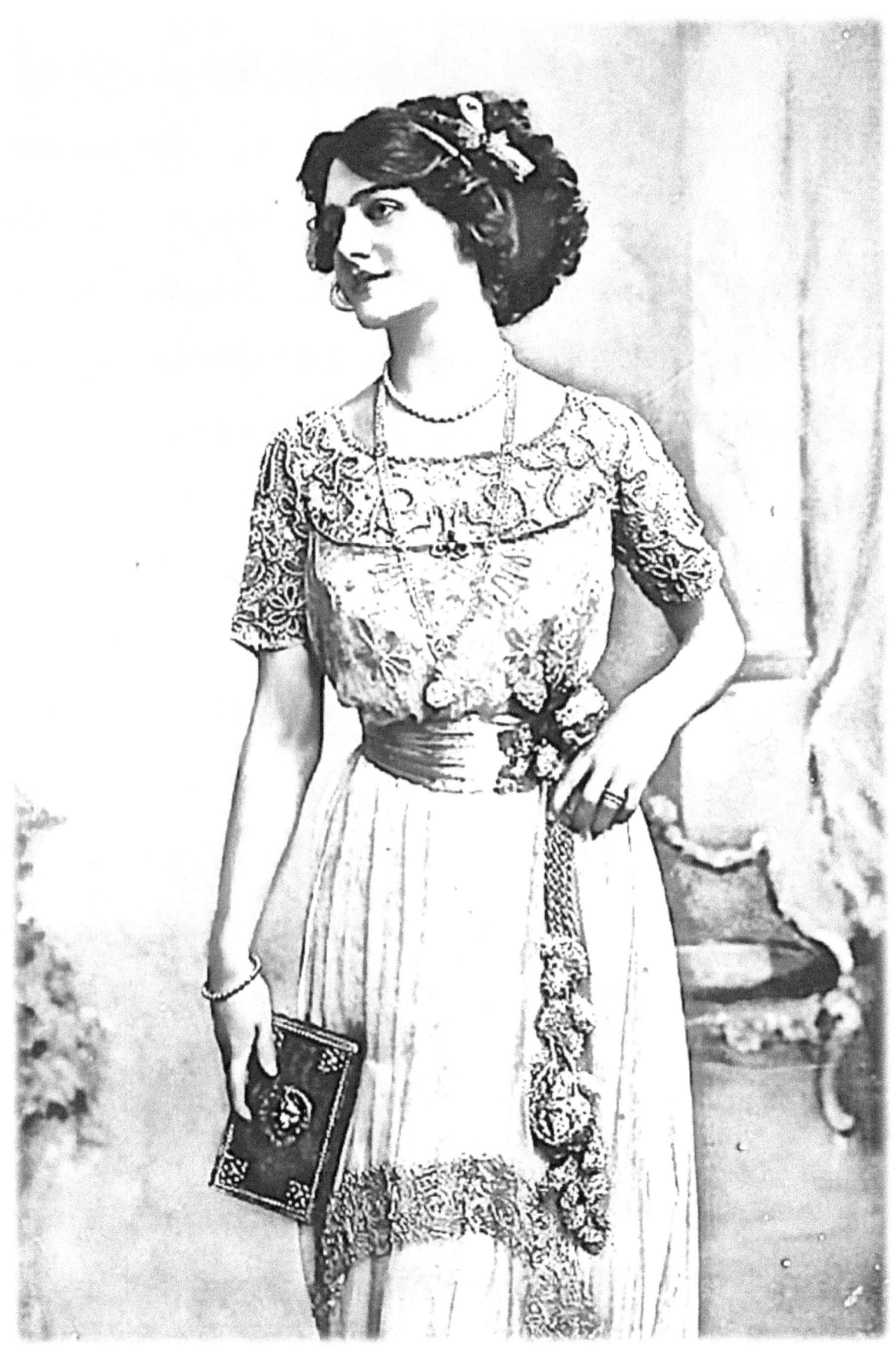

LILY ELSIE

15

LILY ELSIE, Actress & Singer 1886-1964
AMAZON AUTHOR PAGE: http://amzn.to/2g7qeAZ
ETSY SHOP, "JLA" :https://www.janetlongarts/shop/Etsy.com
ETSY VINTAGE SHOP: https://www.etsy.com/shop/AdoptionsLtd

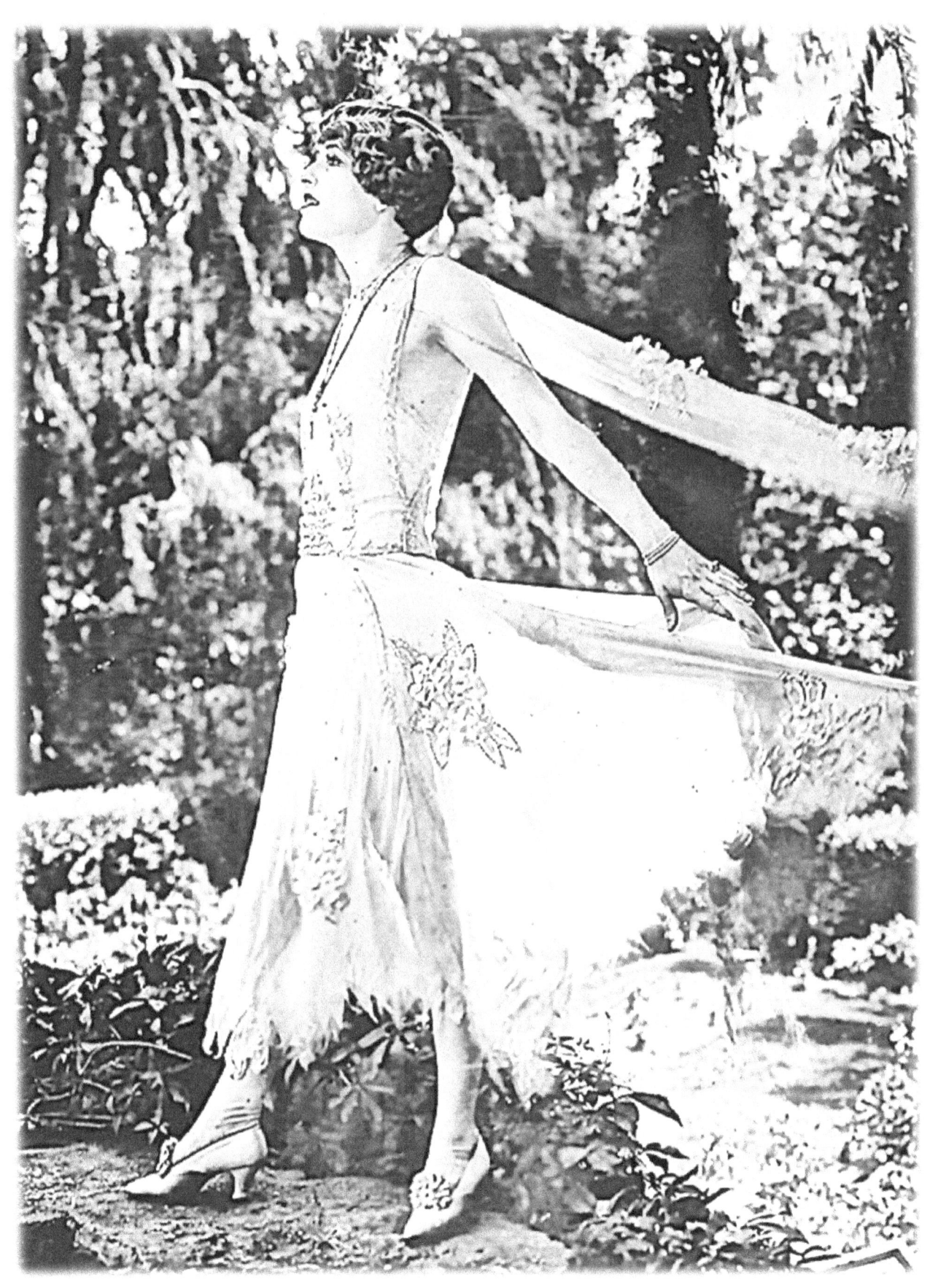

CLAIR WINDSOR 1892-1972

CLAIR WINDSOR 1892-1972 Silent Films
AMAZON AUTHOR PAGE: http://amzn.to/2g7qeAZ

ETSY SHOP, "JLA" :https://www.janetlongarts/shop/Etsy.com
ETSY VINTAGE SHOP: https://www.etsy.com/shop/AdoptionsLtd

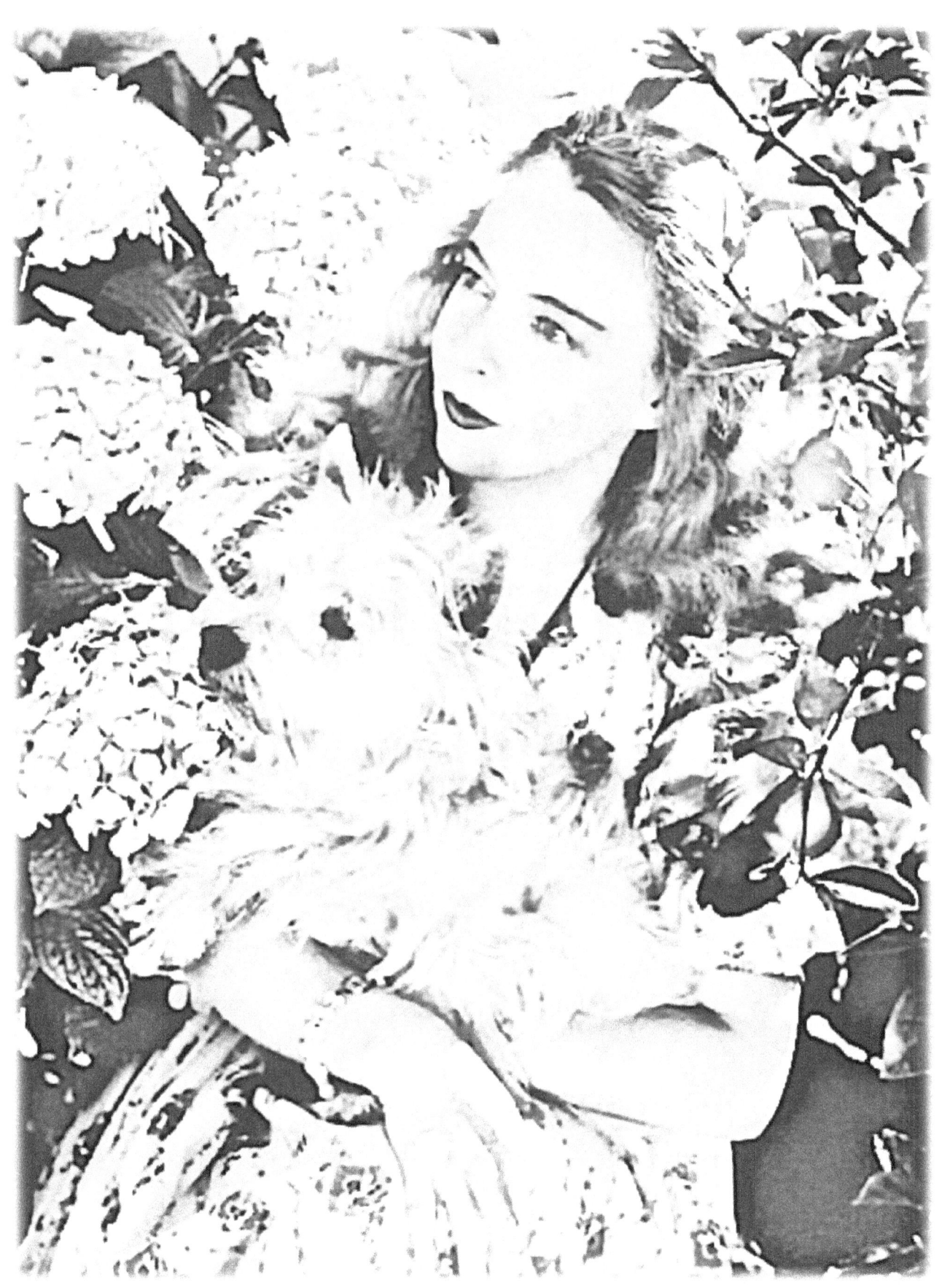

LILIAN GISH & HER DOG

LILIAN GISH & HER DOG 1893-1993
AMAZON AUTHOR PAGE: http://amzn.to/2g7qeAZ

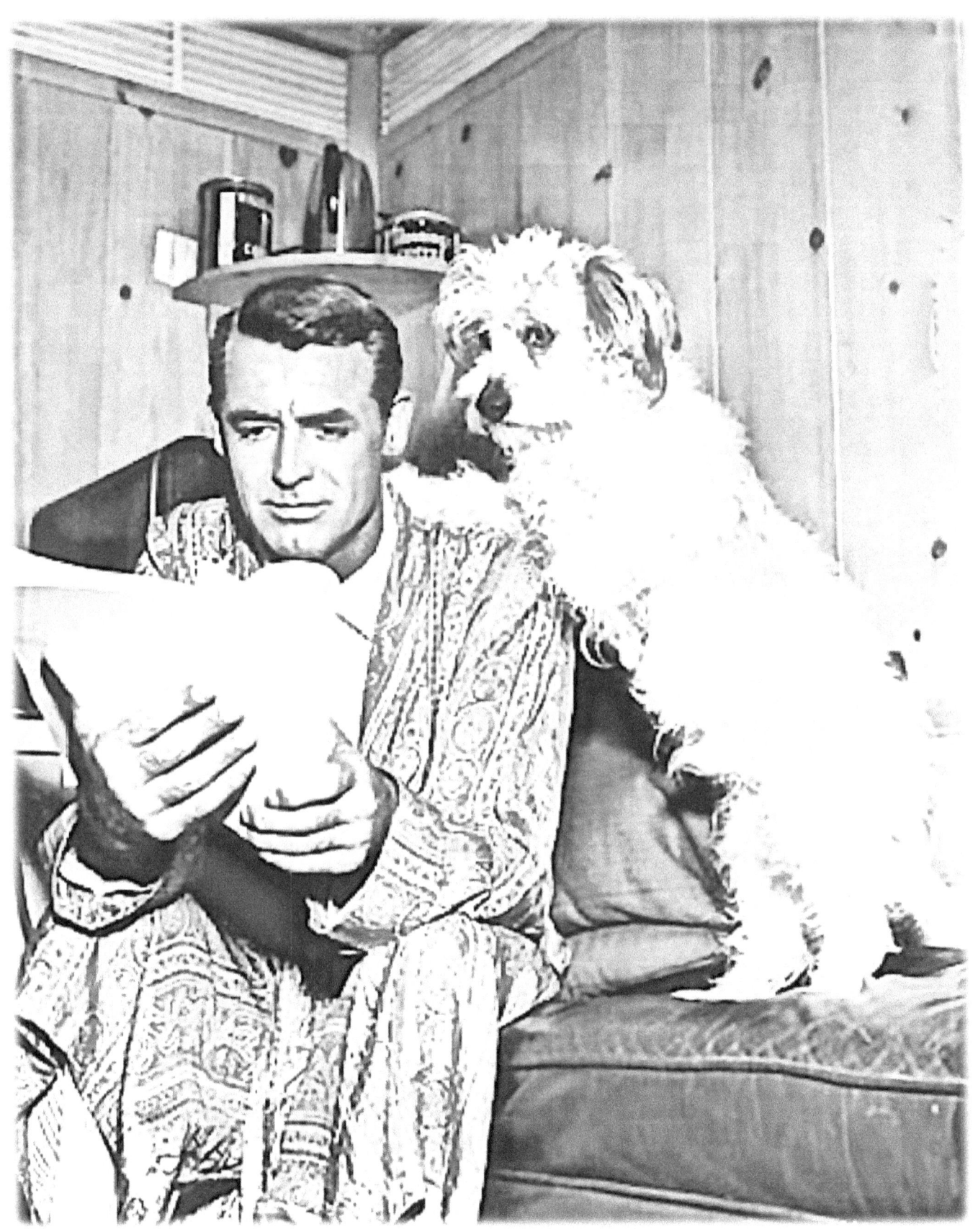

CARY GRANT

CARY GRANT

AMAZON AUTHOR PAGE: http://amzn.to/2g7qeAZ
ETSY SHOP, "JLA" :https://www.janetlongarts/shop/Etsy.com
ETSY VINTAGE SHOP: https://www.etsy.com/shop/AdoptionsLtd

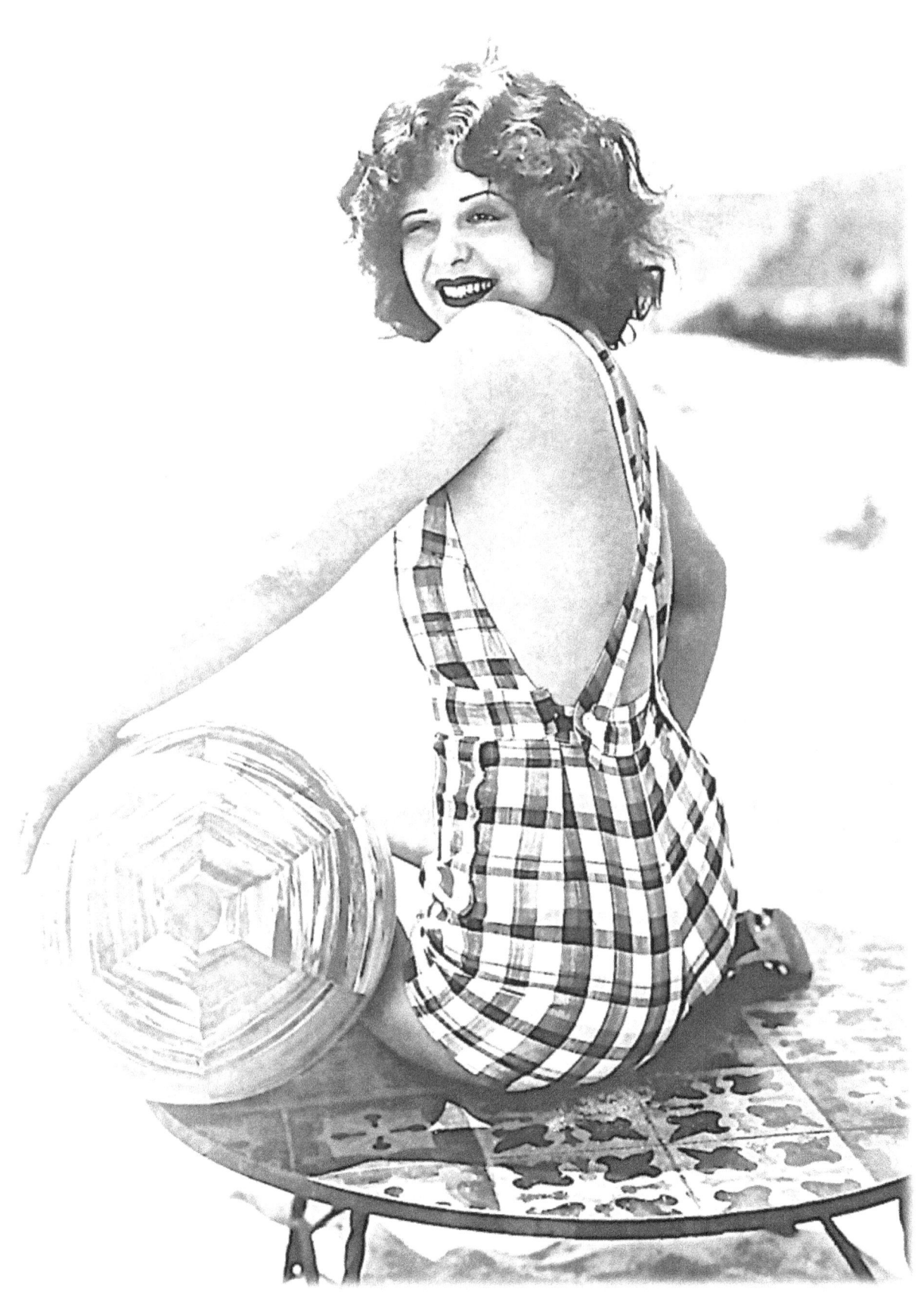

CLARA BOW [1920]   1905-1965

CLARA BOW [1920] 1905-1965
AMAZON AUTHOR PAGE: http://amzn.to/2g7qeAZ

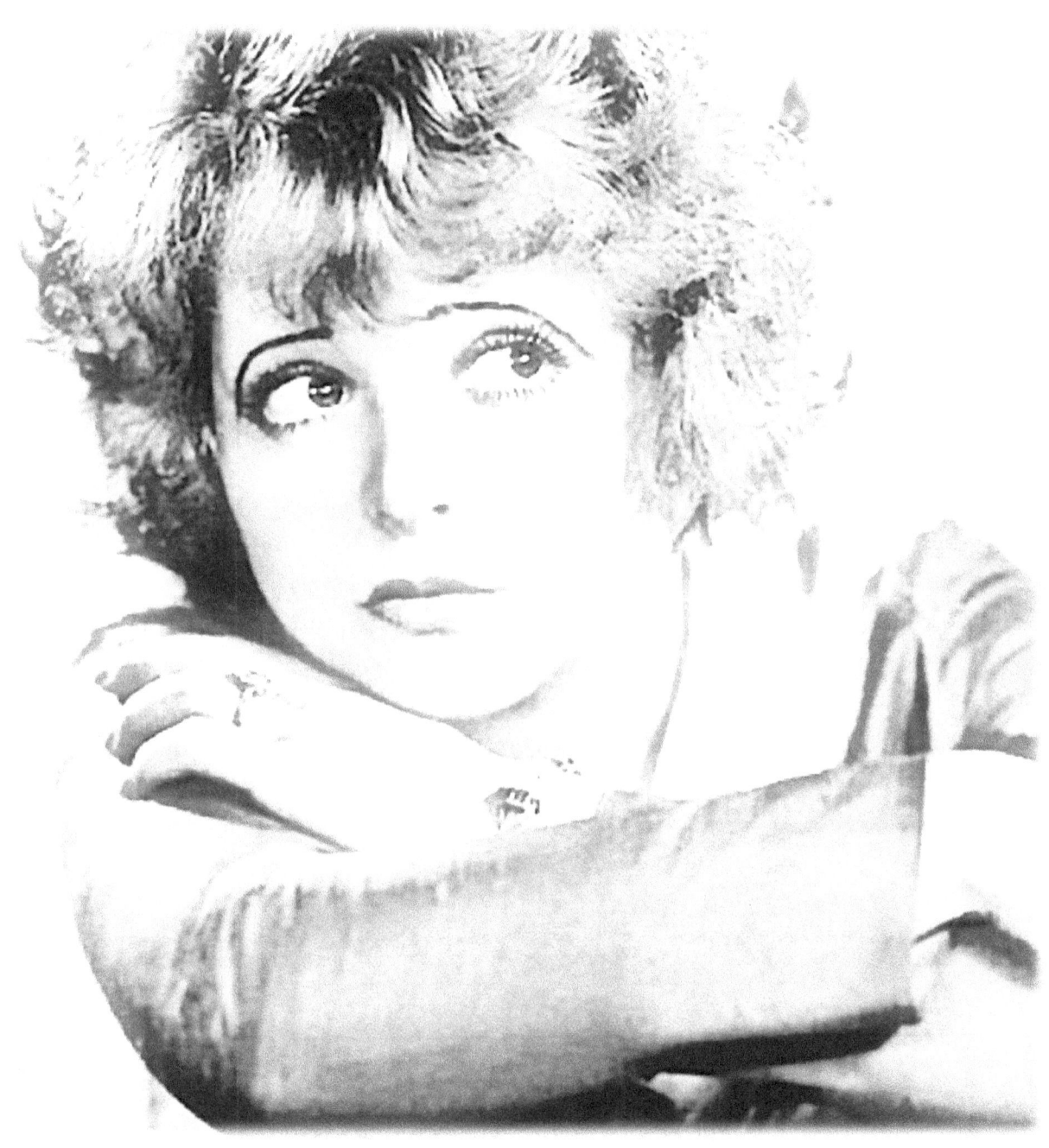

CLARA BOW

CLARA BOW [1920] 1905-1965
AMAZON AUTHOR PAGE: http://amzn.to/2g7qeAZ

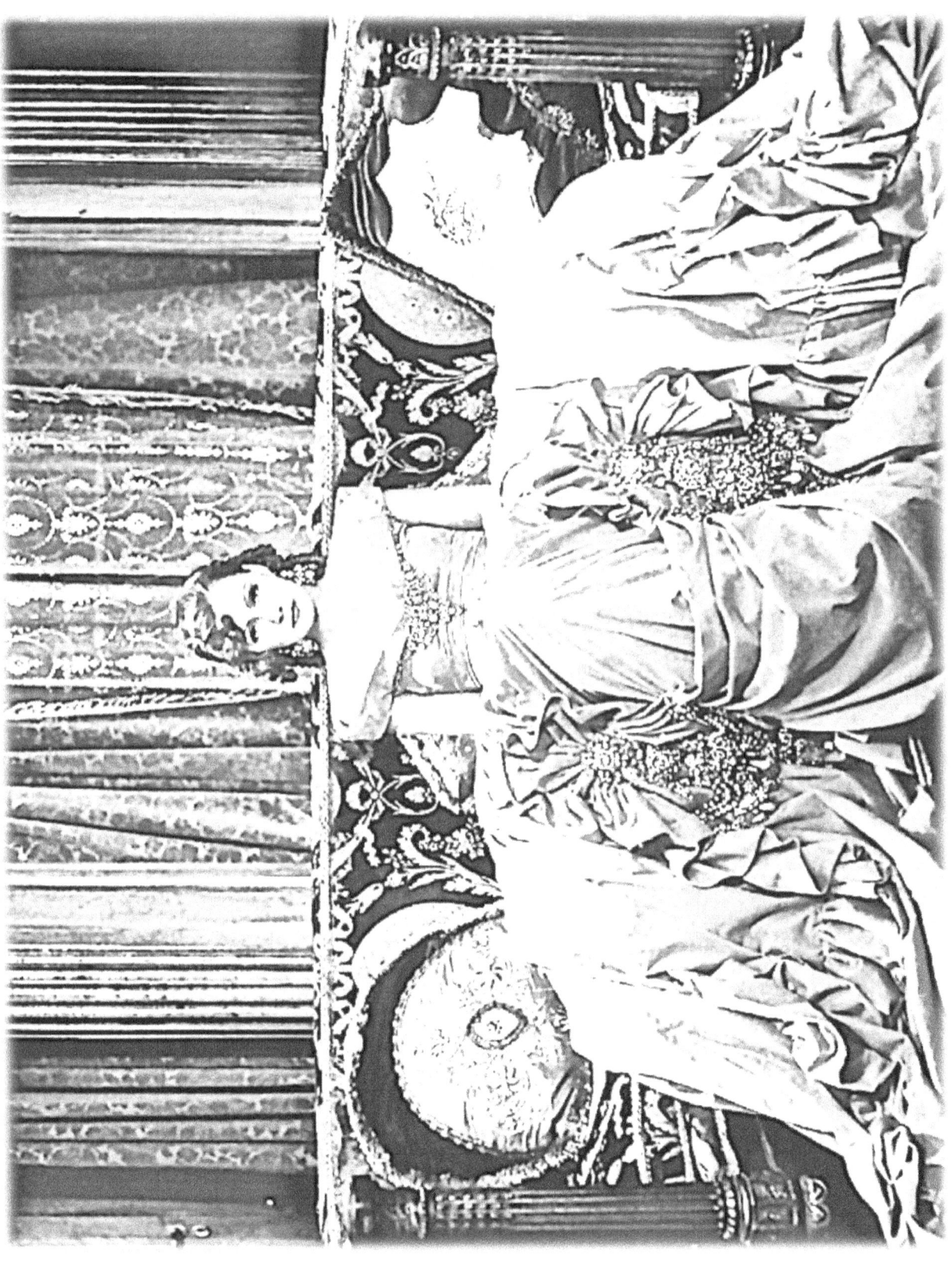

GRETA GARBO

GRETA GARBO 1905-1990

AMAZON AUTHOR PAGE: http://amzn.to/2g7qeAZ

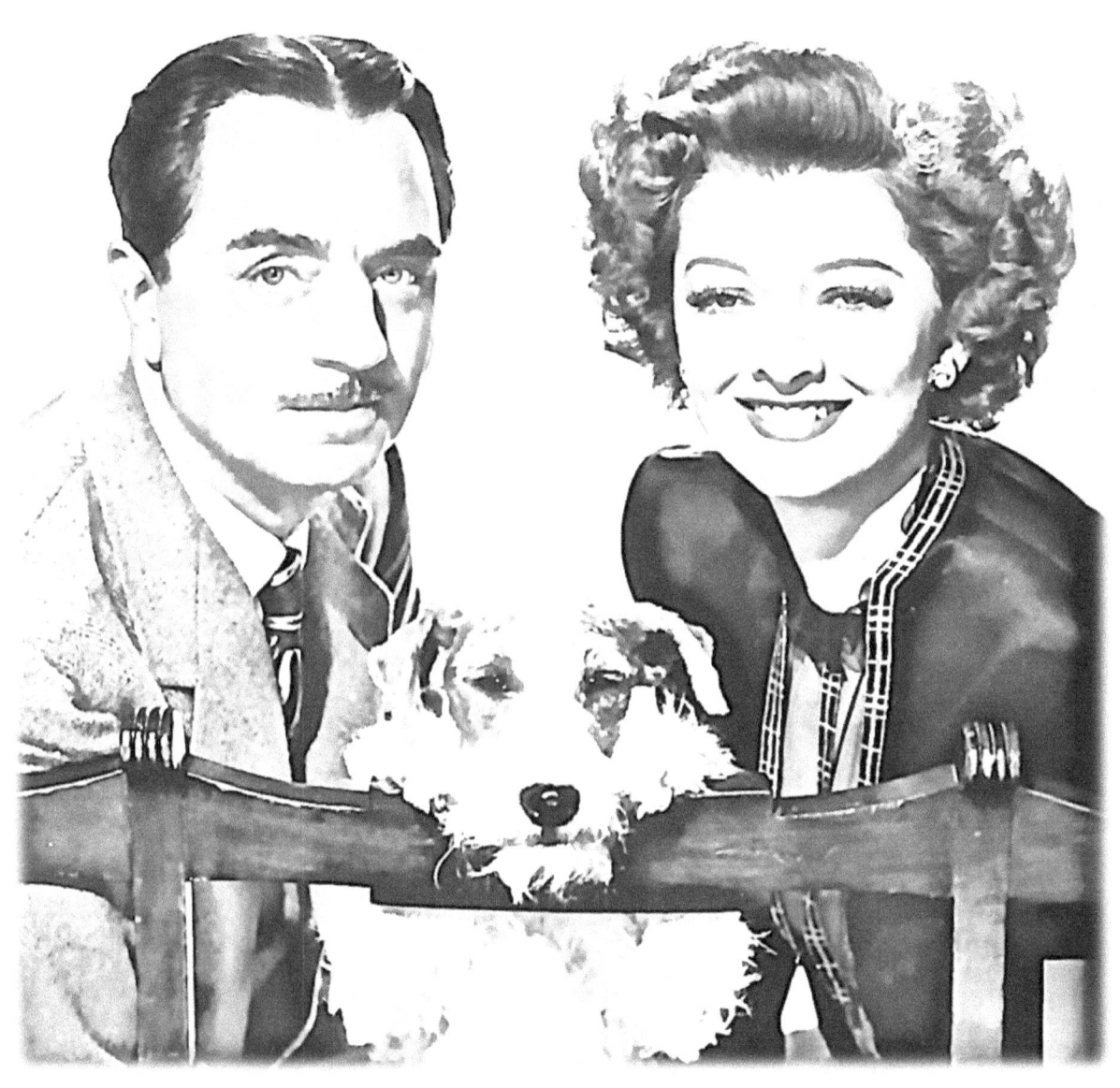

MYRNA LOY, WILLIAM POWELL & ASTA
The Thin Man

MYRNA LOY, WILLIAM POWELL & ASTA **1905-1993**
AMAZON AUTHOR PAGE: http://amzn.to/2g7qeAZ
ETSY SHOP, "JLA" :https://www.janetlongarts/shop/Etsy.com
ETSY VINTAGE SHOP: https://www.etsy.com/shop/AdoptionsLtd

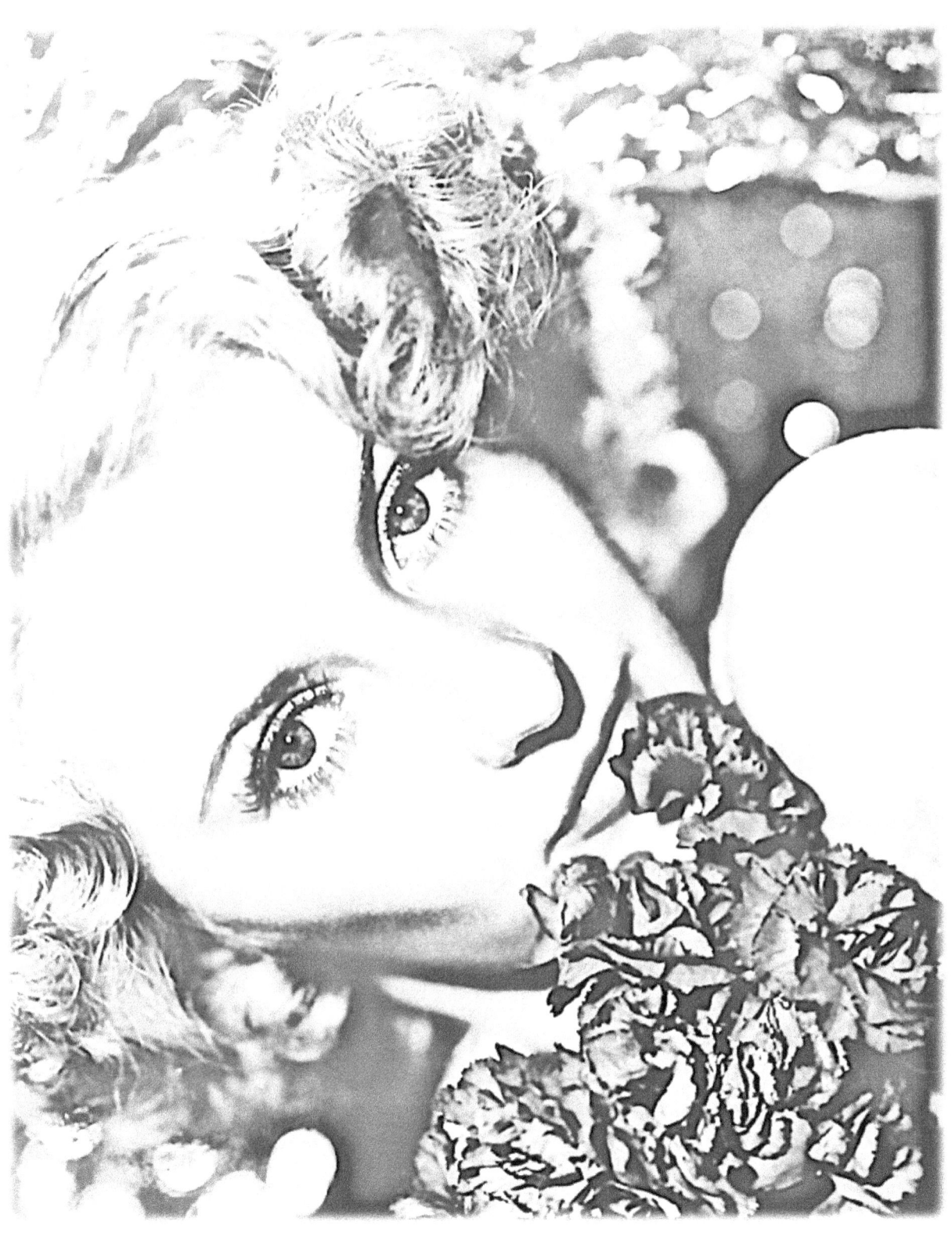

BARBARA STANWYK

BARBARA STANWYCK 1907-1990
AMAZON AUTHOR PAGE: http://amzn.to/2g7qeAZ
ETSY SHOP, "JLA" :https://www.janetlongarts/shop/Etsy.com
ETSY VINTAGE SHOP: https://www.etsy.com/shop/AdoptionsLtd

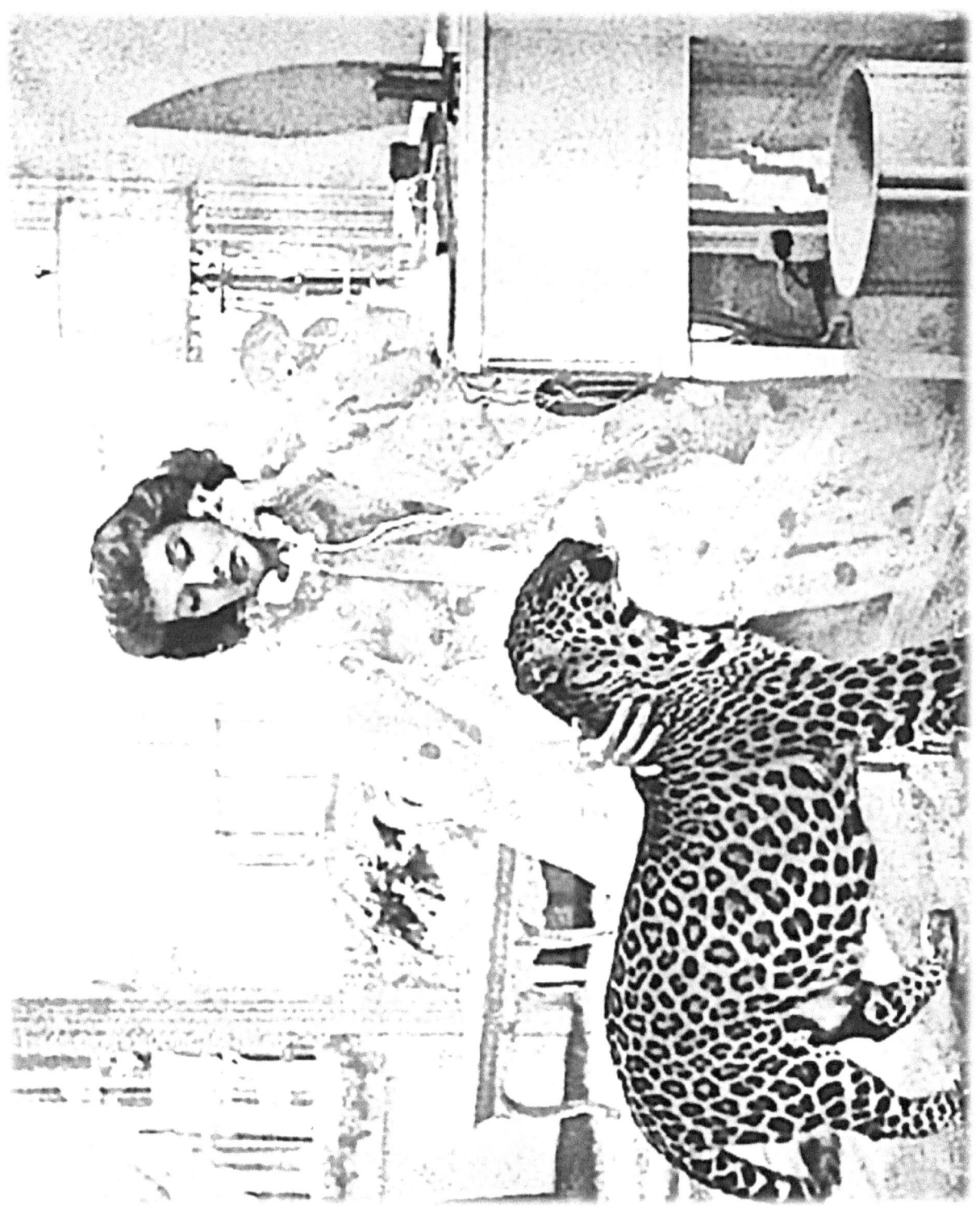

KATHERINE HEPBURN

KATHERINE HEPBURN **1907-1990**
'Bringing Up Baby"
AMAZON AUTHOR PAGE: http://amzn.to/2g7qeAZ

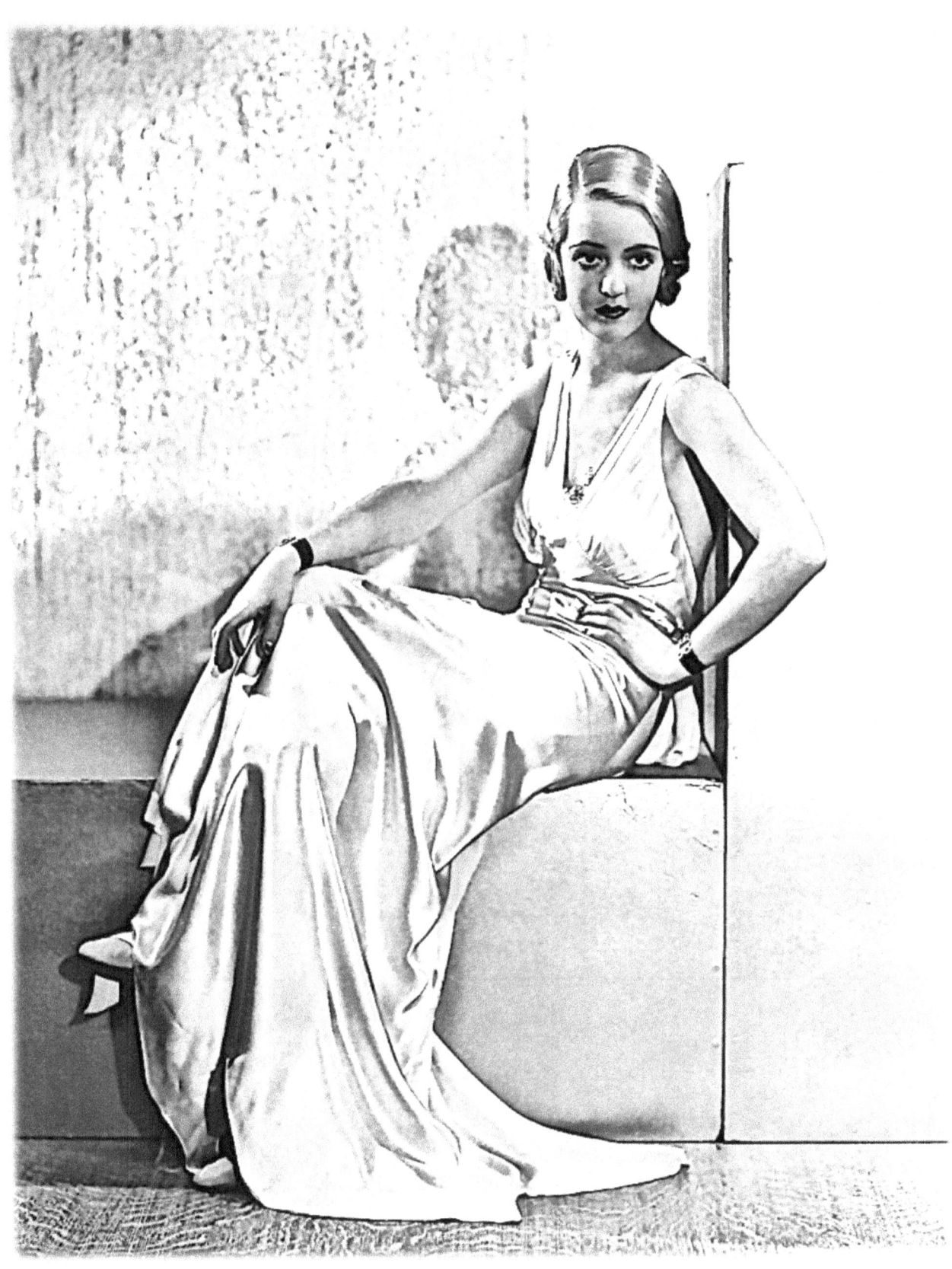

BETTE DAVIS

BETTE DAVIS 1907-2003
AMAZON AUTHOR PAGE: http://amzn.to/2g7qeAZ
ETSY SHOP, "JLA" :https://www.janetlongarts/shop/Etsy.com
ETSY VINTAGE SHOP: https://www.etsy.com/shop/AdoptionsLtd

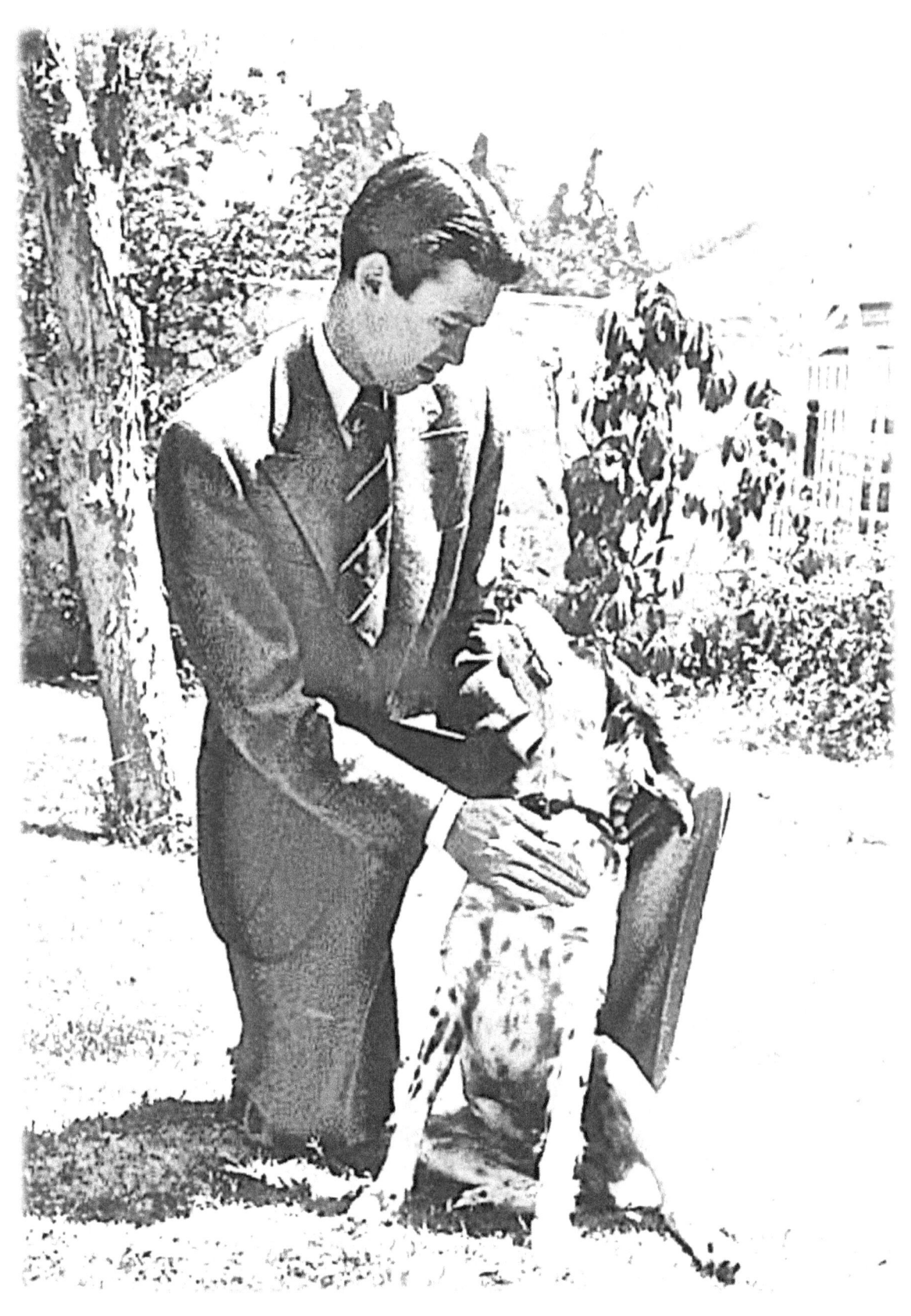

JIMMY STEWART & BEAU

JIMMY STEWART & BEAU
AMAZON AUTHOR PAGE: http://amzn.to/2g7qeAZ

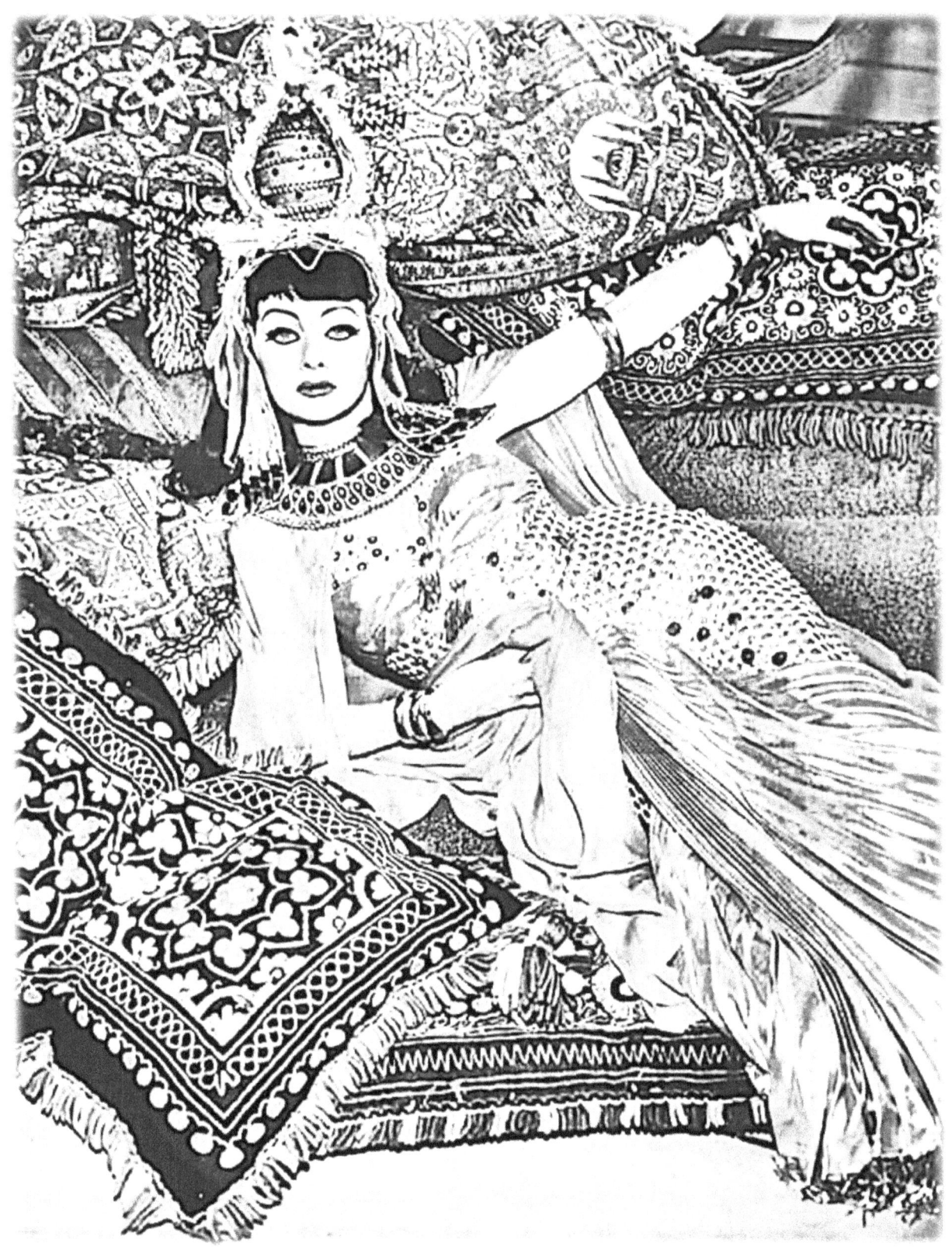

LUCILLE BALL

LUCILLE BALL as CLEOPATRA 1911-1989
AMAZON AUTHOR PAGE: http://amzn.to/2g7qeAZ

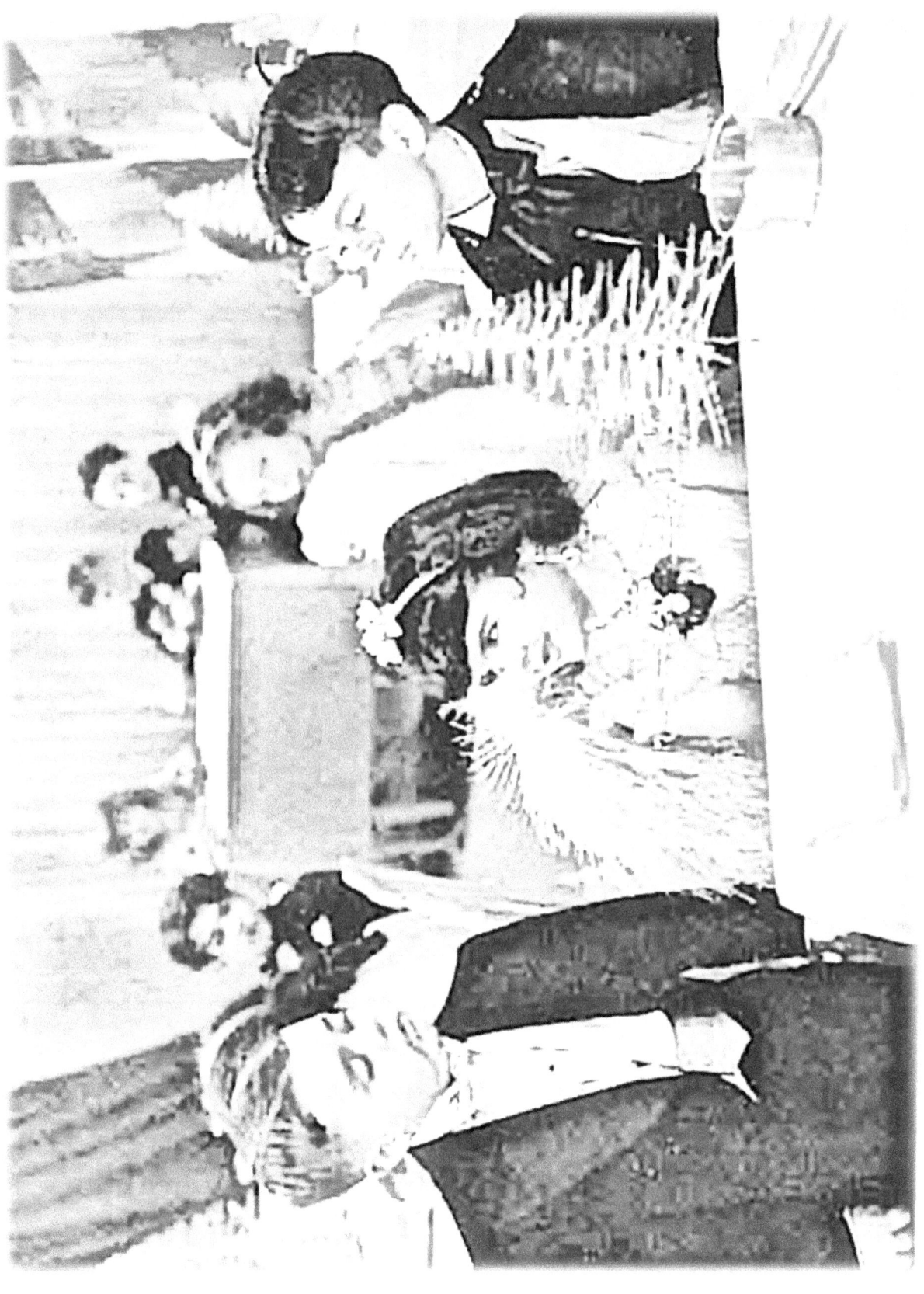

SPANKY, DARLA & ALFALFA

Little Rascals 1931 SPANKY, DARLA & ALFALFA
AMAZON AUTHOR PAGE: http://amzn.to/2g7qeAZ

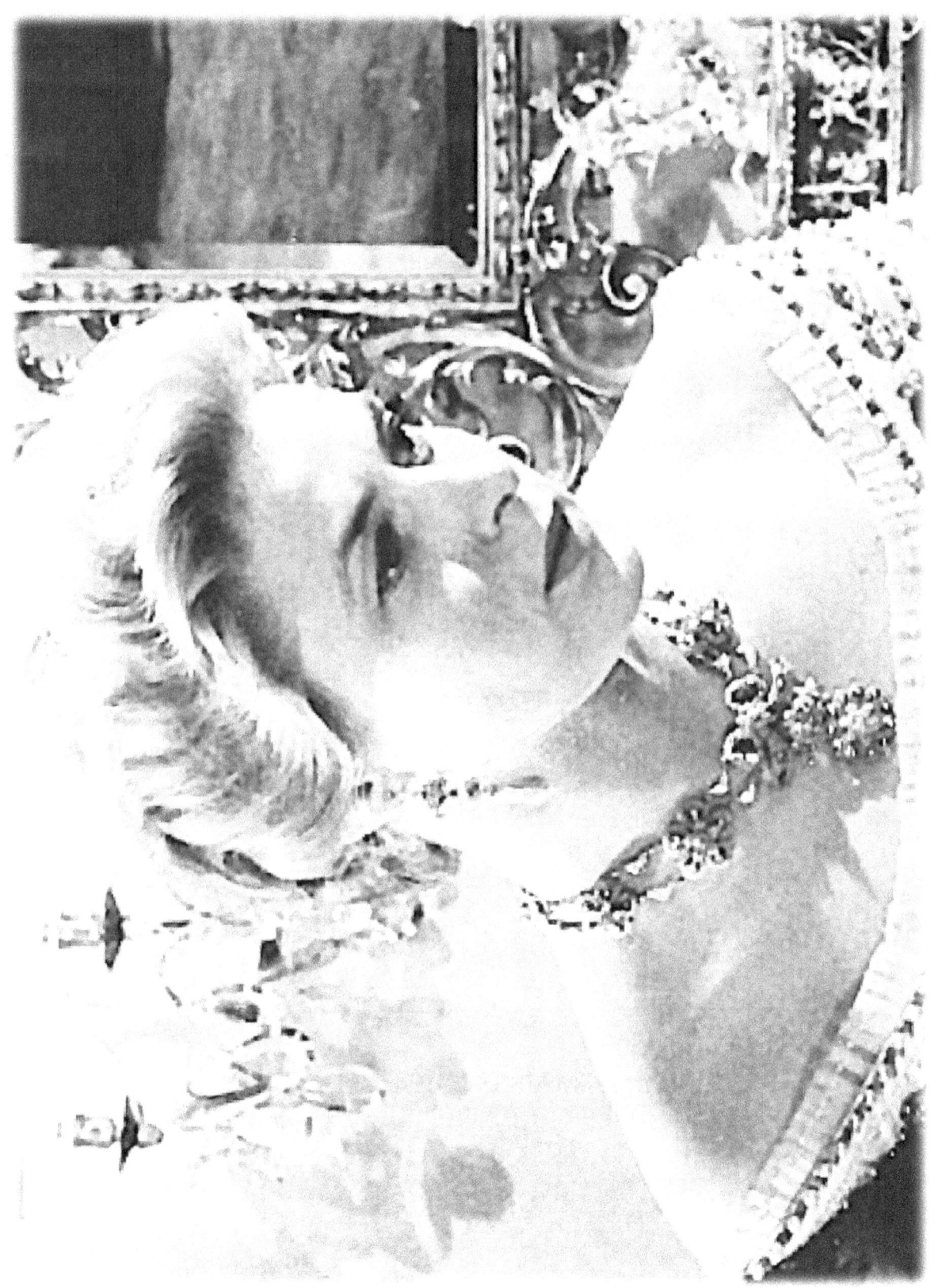

INGRID BERGMAN as ANASTASIA

INGRID BERGMAN 1915-1982 as ANESTASIA
AMAZON AUTHOR PAGE: http://amzn.to/2g7qeAZ

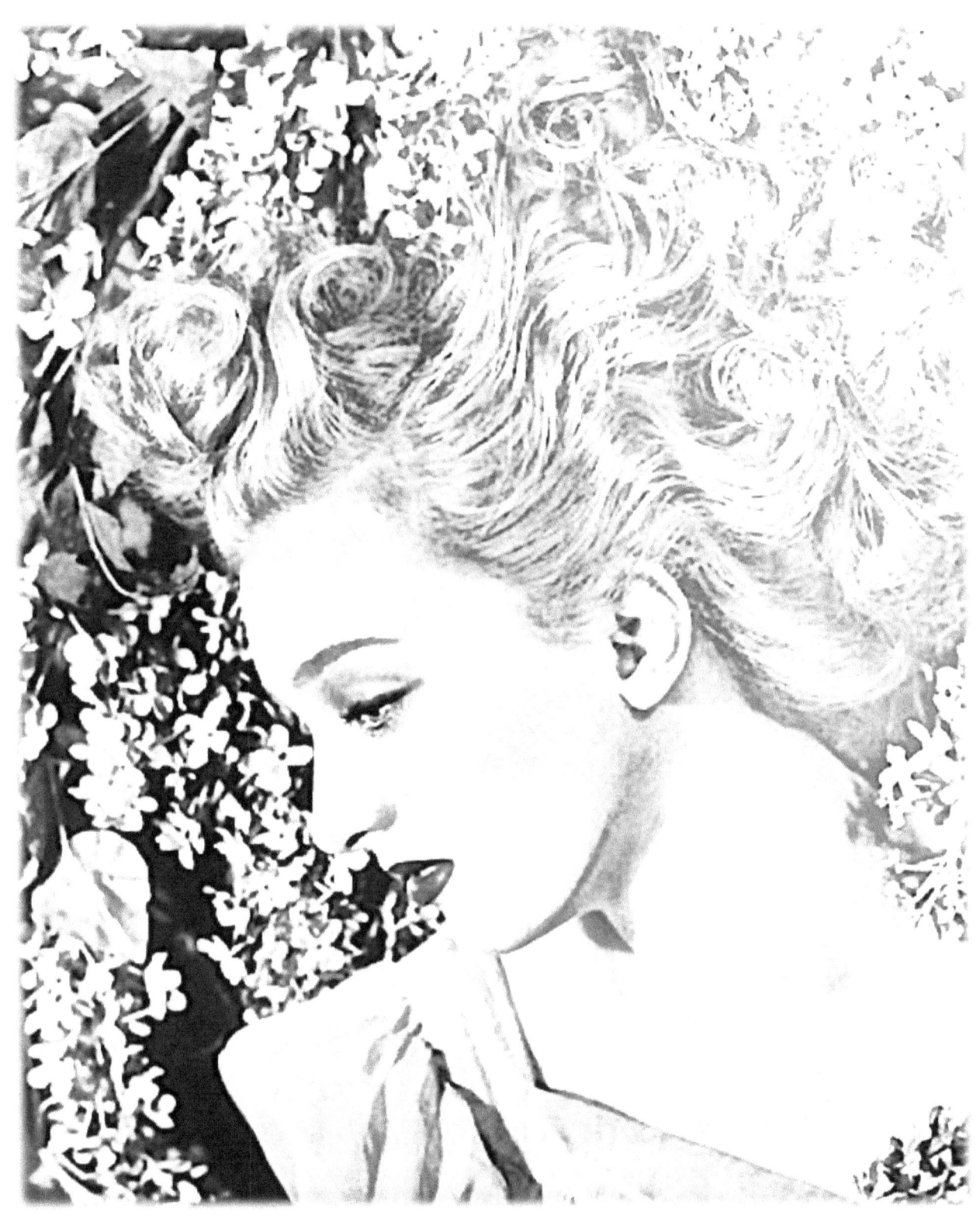

CELESTE HOLM

CELESTE HOLM 1917-2012
AMAZON AUTHOR PAGE: http://amzn.to/2g7qeAZ

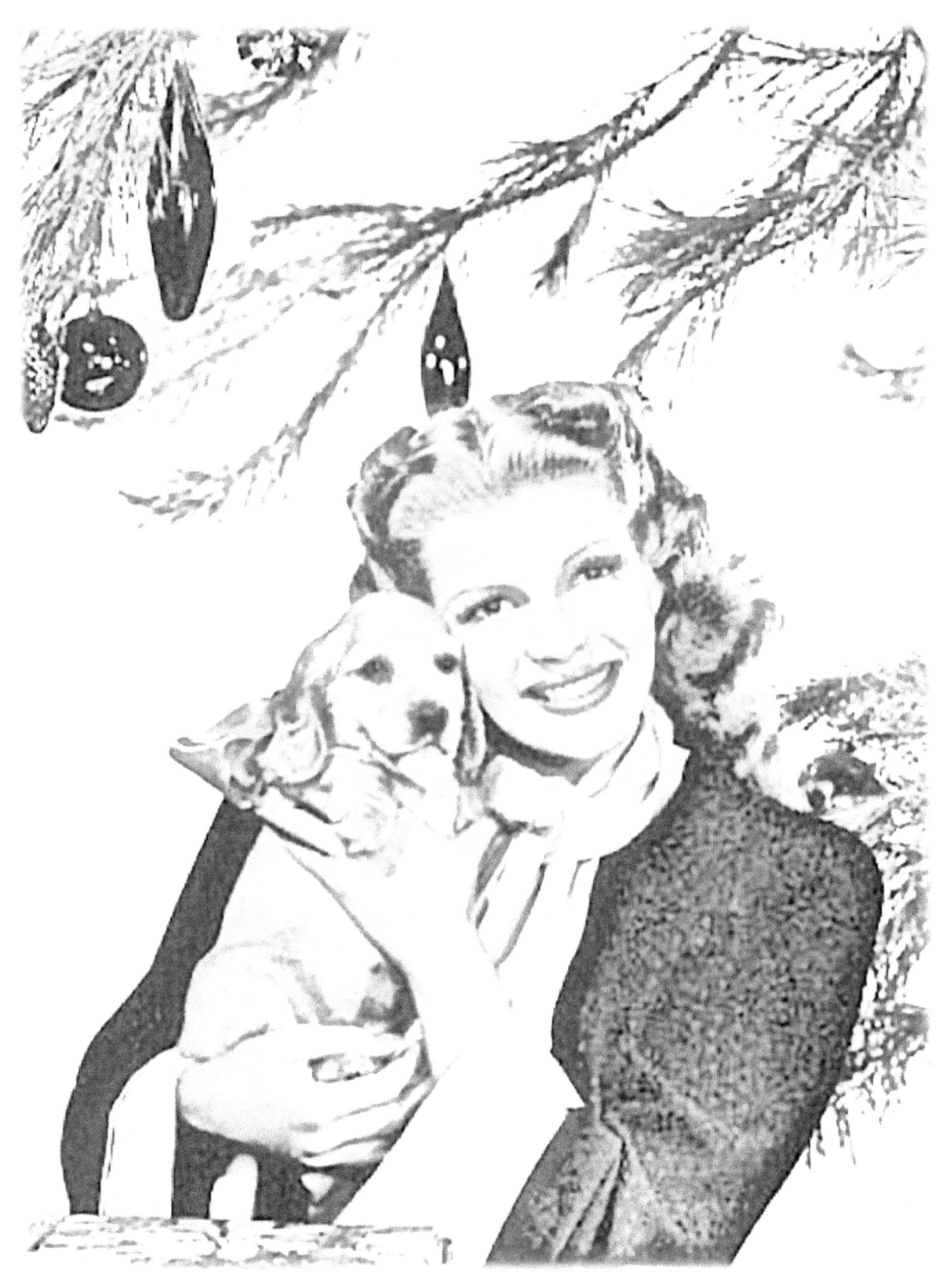

RITA HAYWORTH 1918-1987 & DOG

RITA HAYWORTH 1918-1987 & DOG
AMAZON AUTHOR PAGE: http://amzn.to/2g7qeAZ

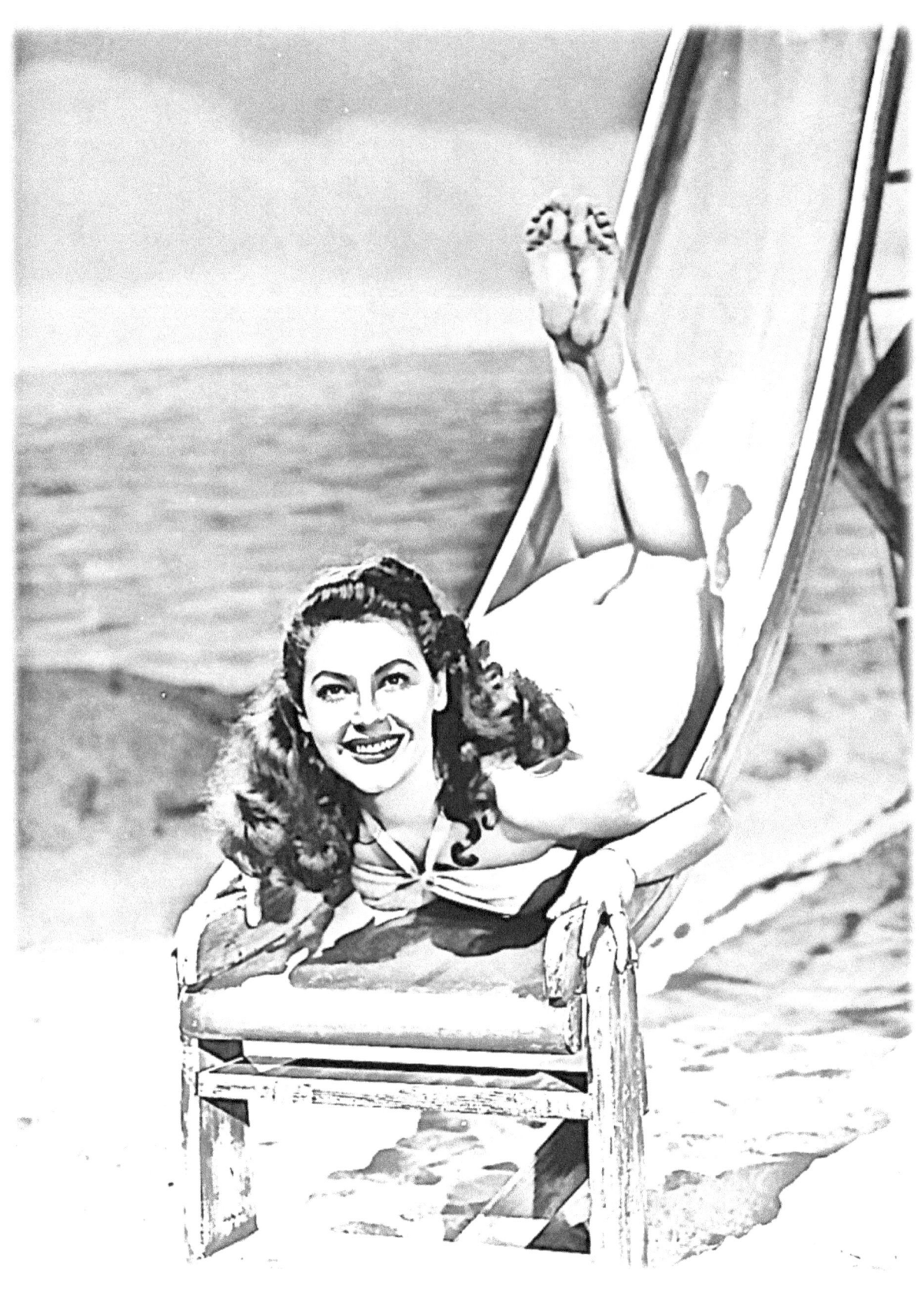

AVA GARDNER

AVA GARDNER 1922-1990
AMAZON AUTHOR PAGE: http://amzn.to/2g7qeAZ
ETSY SHOP, "JLA" :https://www.janetlongarts/shop/Etsy.com
ETSY VINTAGE SHOP: https://www.etsy.com/shop/AdoptionsLtd

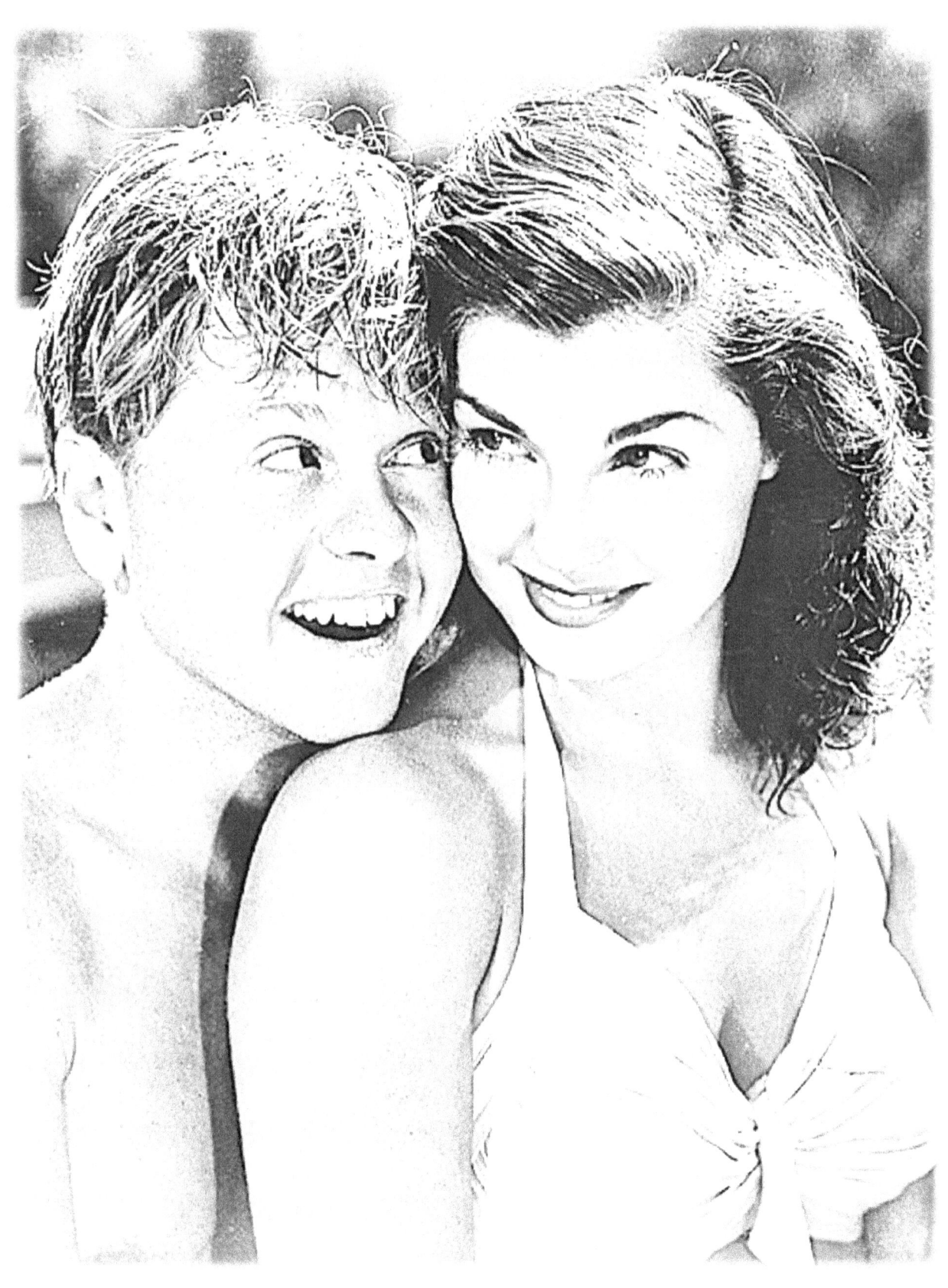

ESTHER **WILLIAMS** & MICKEY ROONEY

**ESTHER WILLIAMS 1921-2013
& MICKEY ROONY 1920 - 2014**

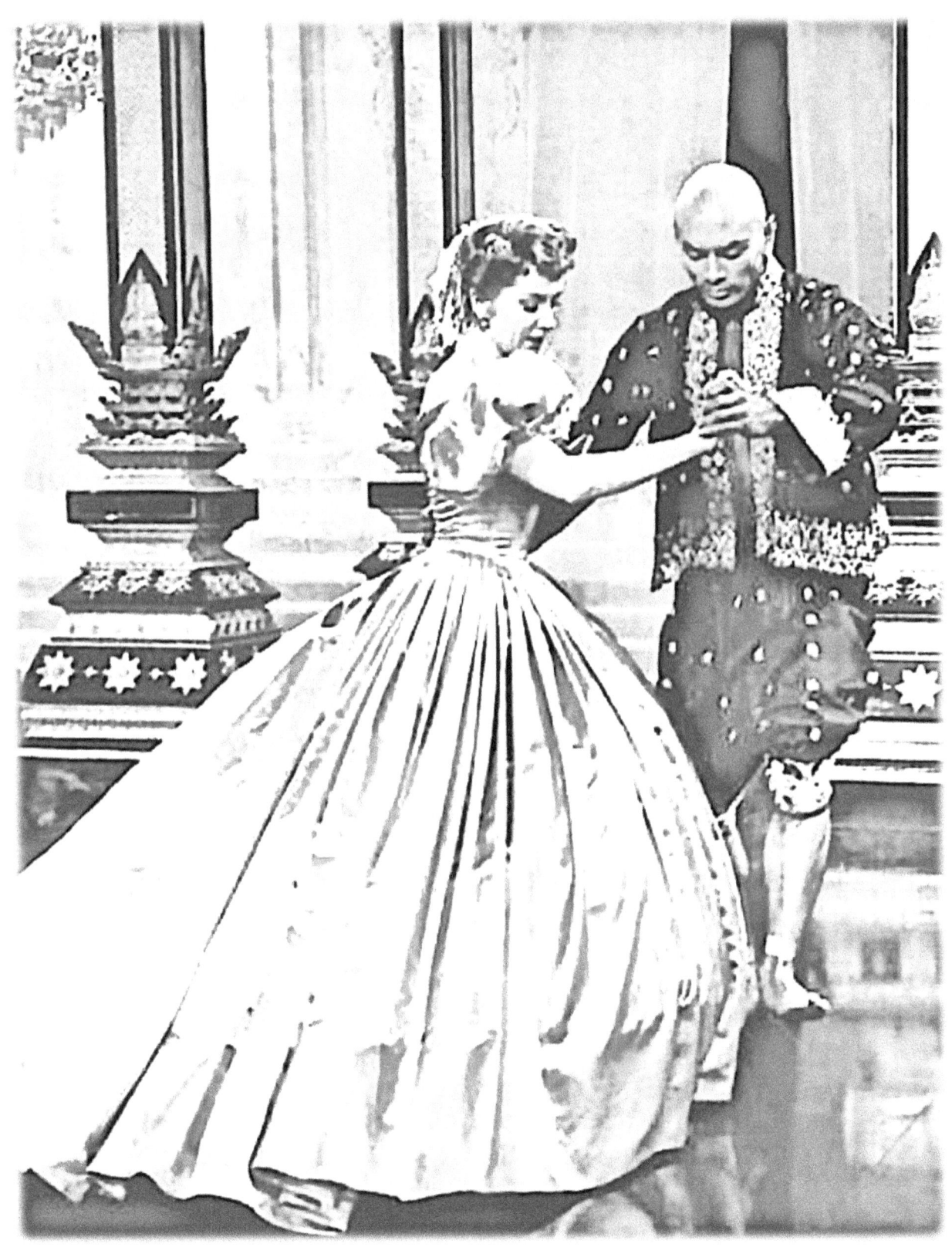

DEBORAH KERR & YUL BRYNNER

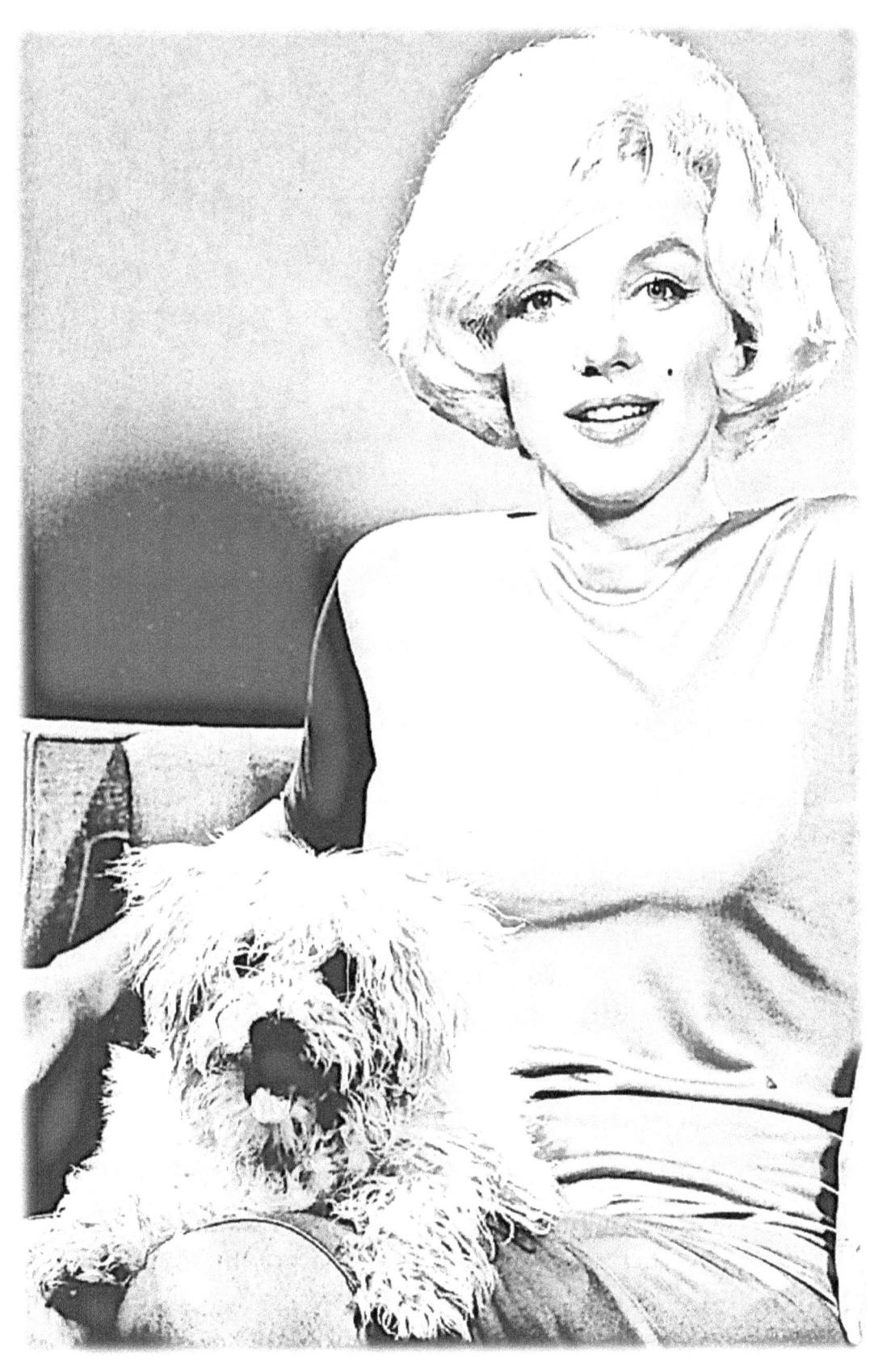

MARILYN MONROE & DOG

MARILYN MONROE 1926-1962 & DOG
AMAZON AUTHOR PAGE: http://amzn.to/2g7qeAZ

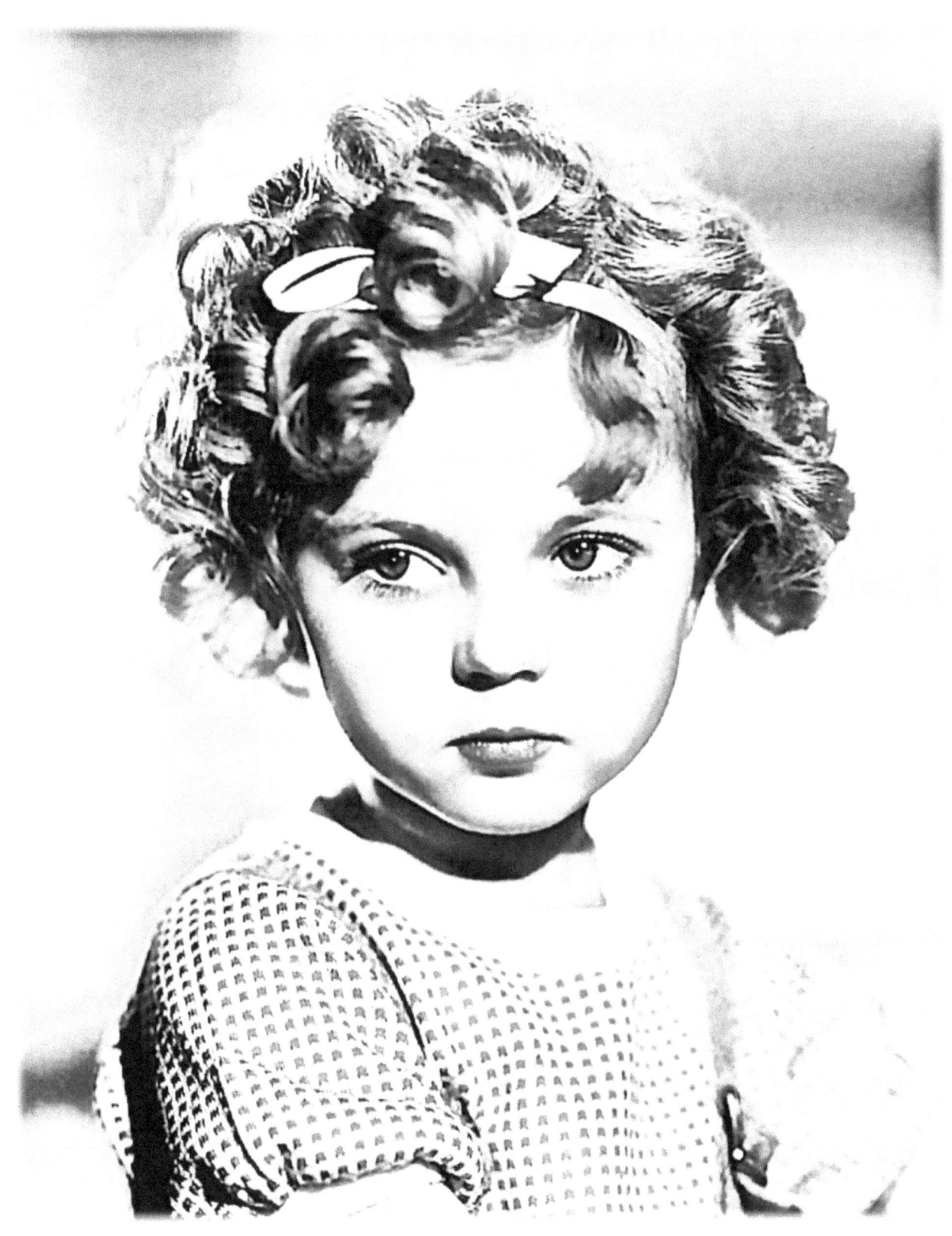

SHIRLEY TEMPLE

SHIRLEY TEMPLE 1928-2014
AMAZON AUTHOR PAGE: http://amzn.to/2g7qeAZ

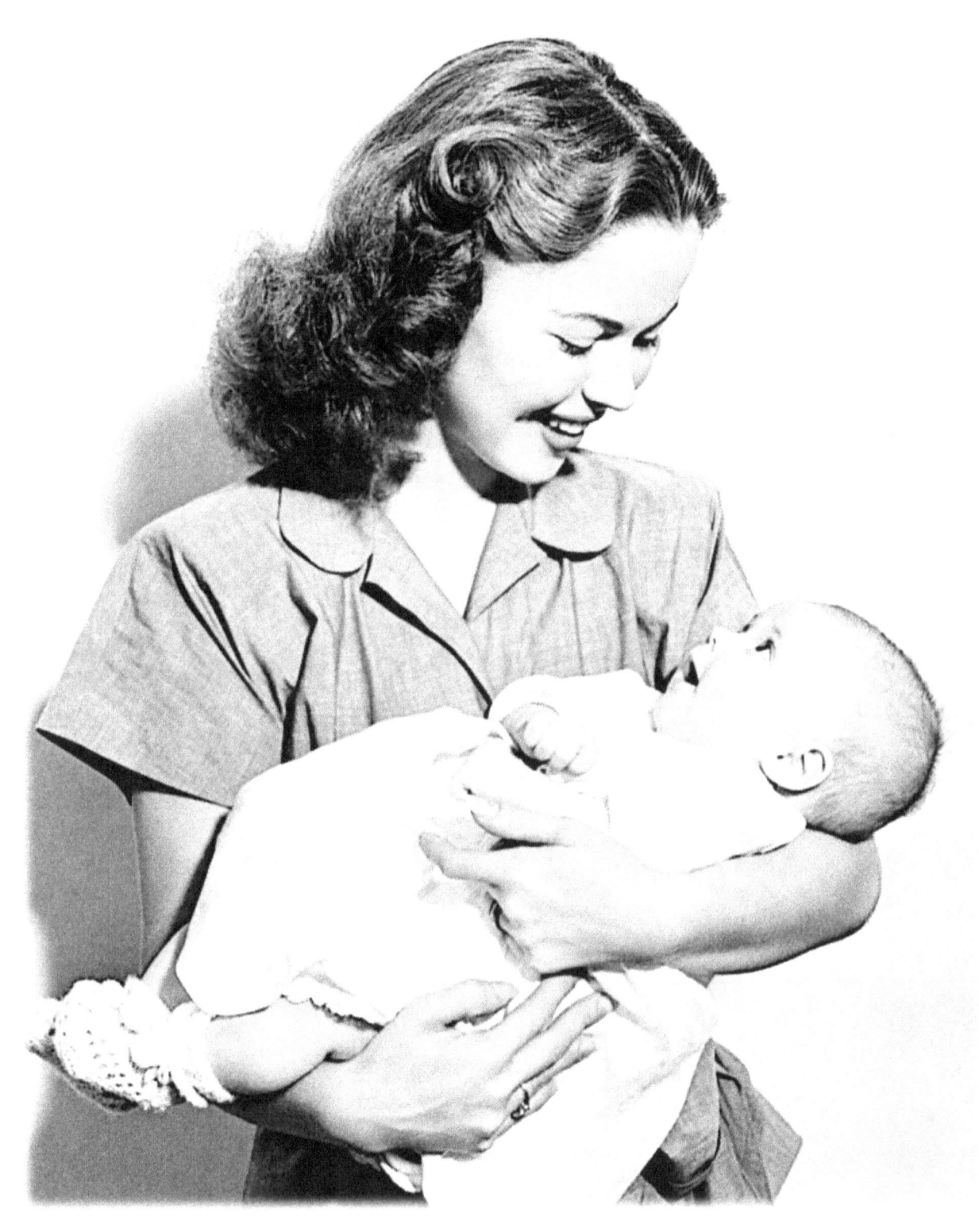

SHIRLEY TEMPLE & HER BABY

SHIRLEY TEMPLE & HER BABY 1928-2014
AMAZON AUTHOR PAGE: http://amzn.to/2g7qeAZ
ETSY SHOP, "JLA" :https://www.janetlongarts/shop/Etsy.com
ETSY VINTAGE SHOP: https://www.etsy.com/shop/AdoptionsLtd

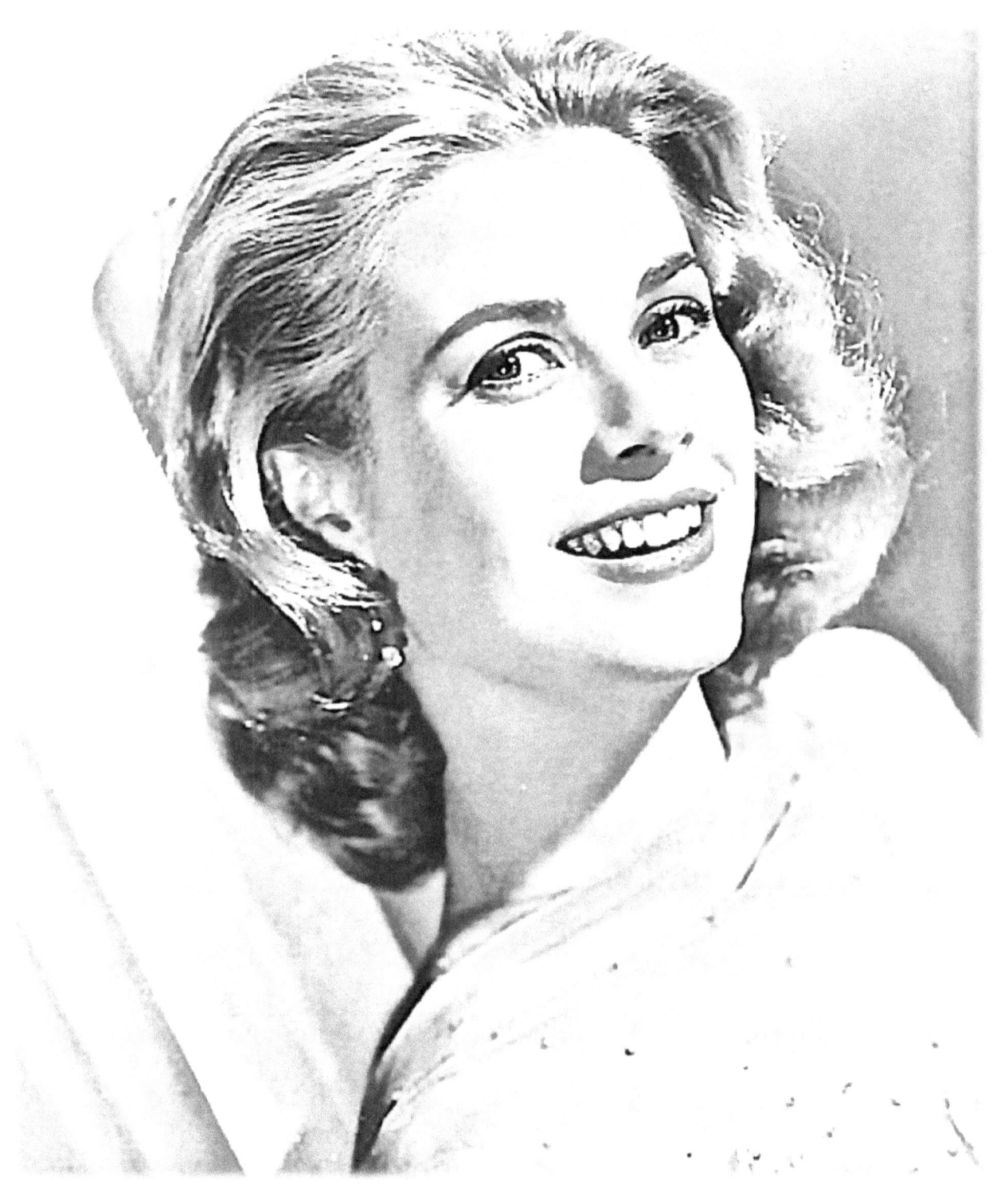

GRACE KELLY

GRACE KELLY 1929-1982
AMAZON AUTHOR PAGE: http://amzn.to/2g7qeAZ

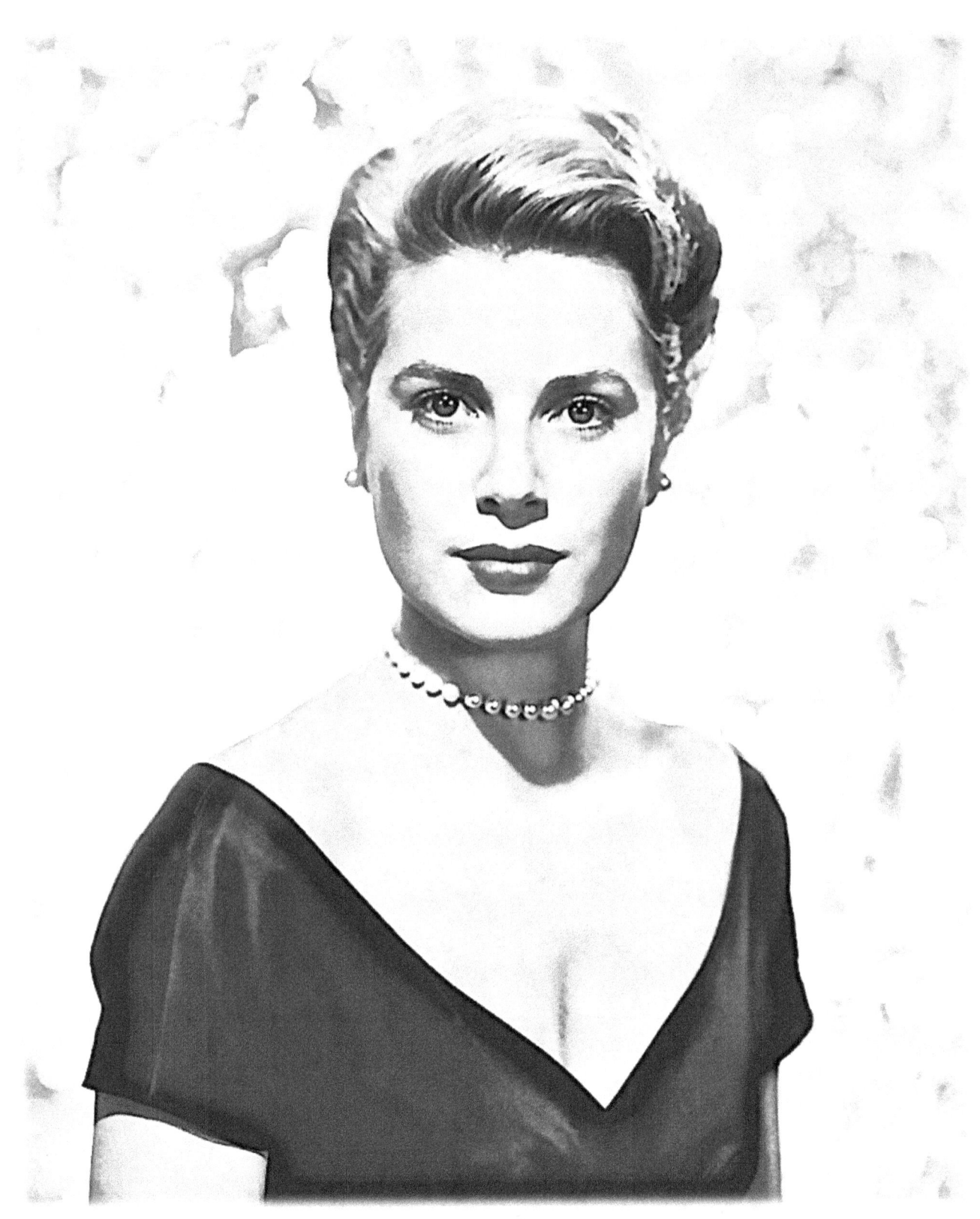

GRACE KELLY

GRACE KELLY 1929-1982
AMAZON AUTHOR PAGE: http://amzn.to/2g7qeAZ

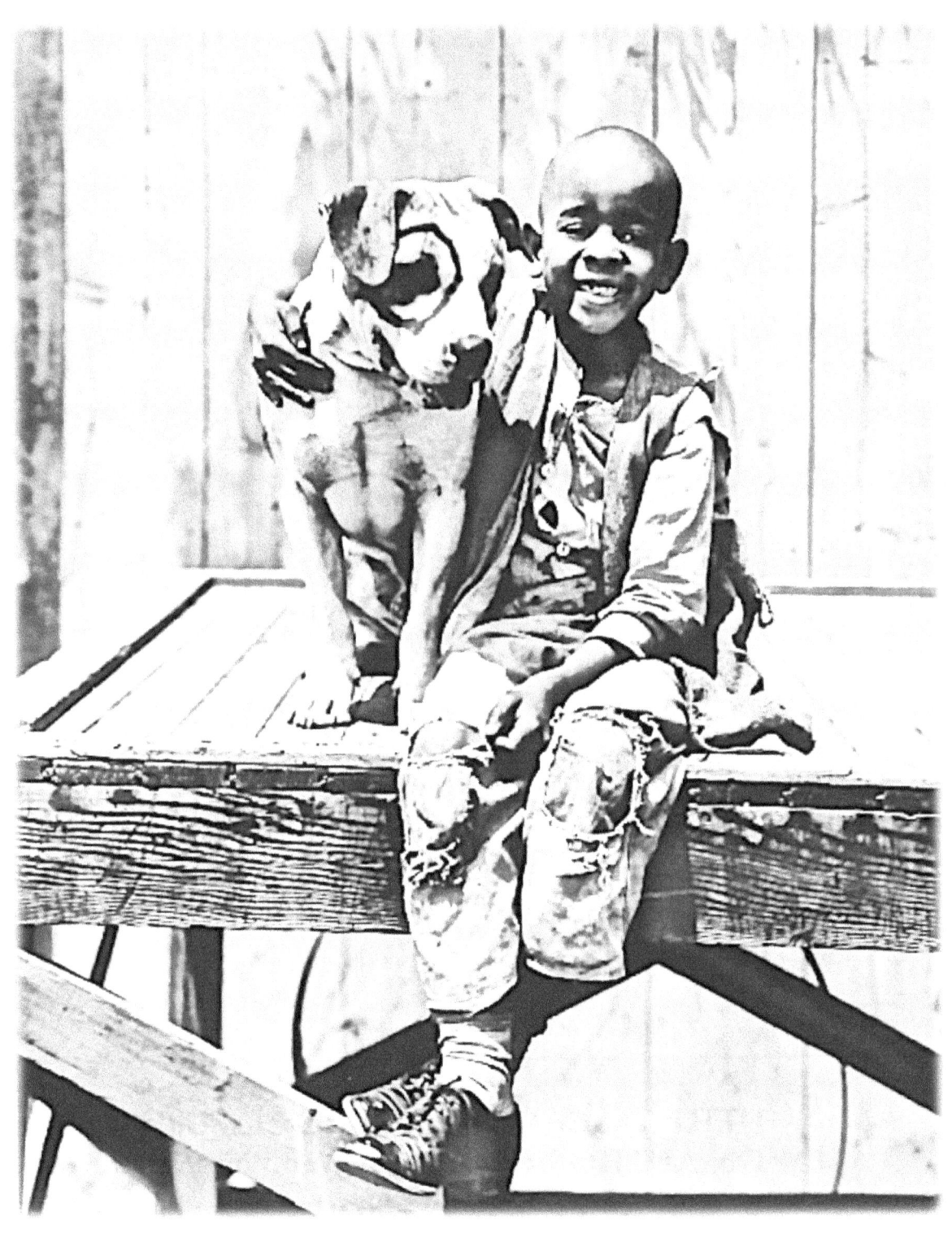

William "Billie" Thomas "BUCKWHEAT"

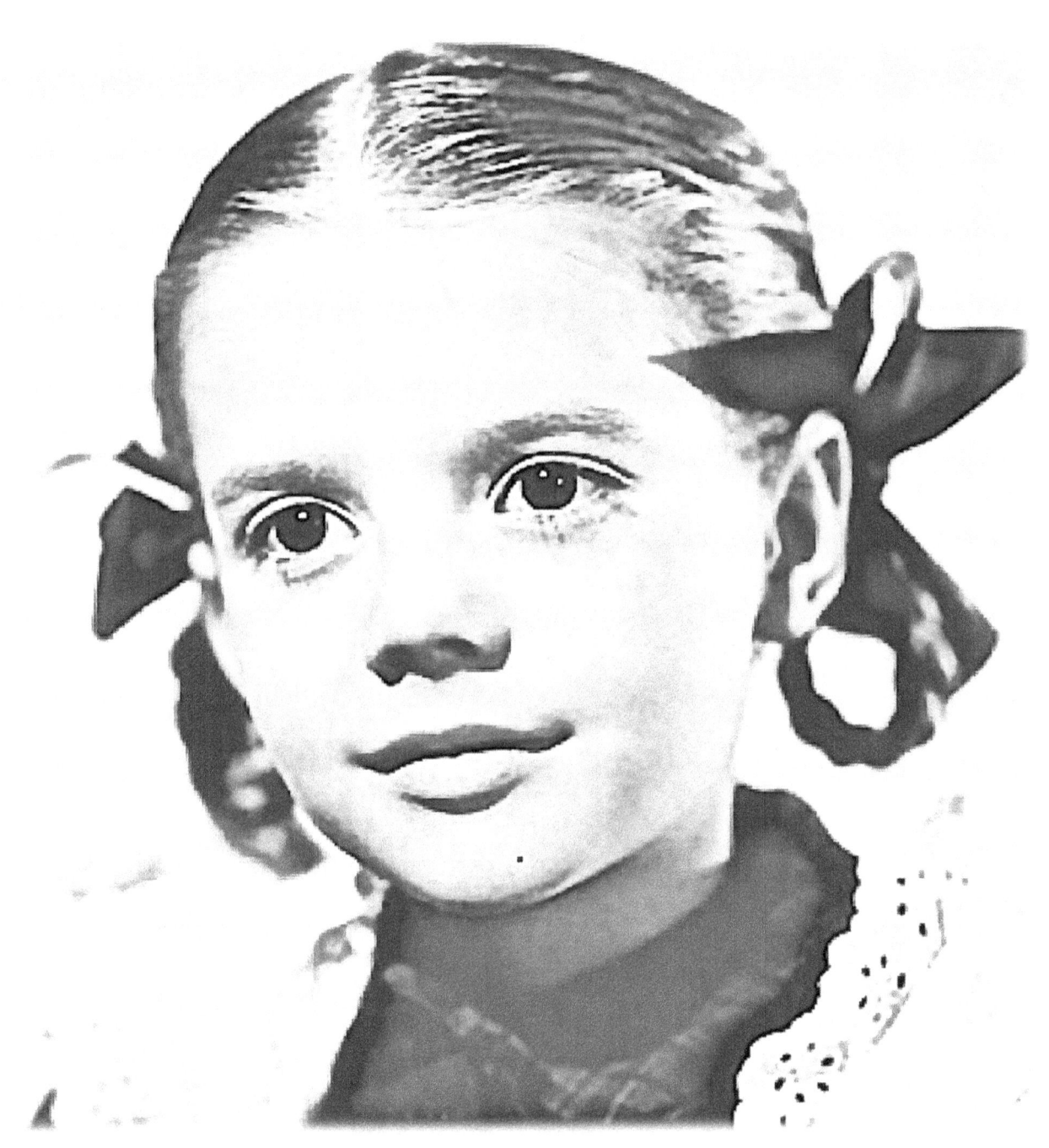

NATALIE WOOD

NATALIE WOOD 1938-1981
AMAZON AUTHOR PAGE: http://amzn.to/2g7qeAZ
ETSY SHOP, "JLA" :https://www.janetlongarts/shop/Etsy.com
ETSY VINTAGE SHOP: https://www.etsy.com/shop/AdoptionsLtd

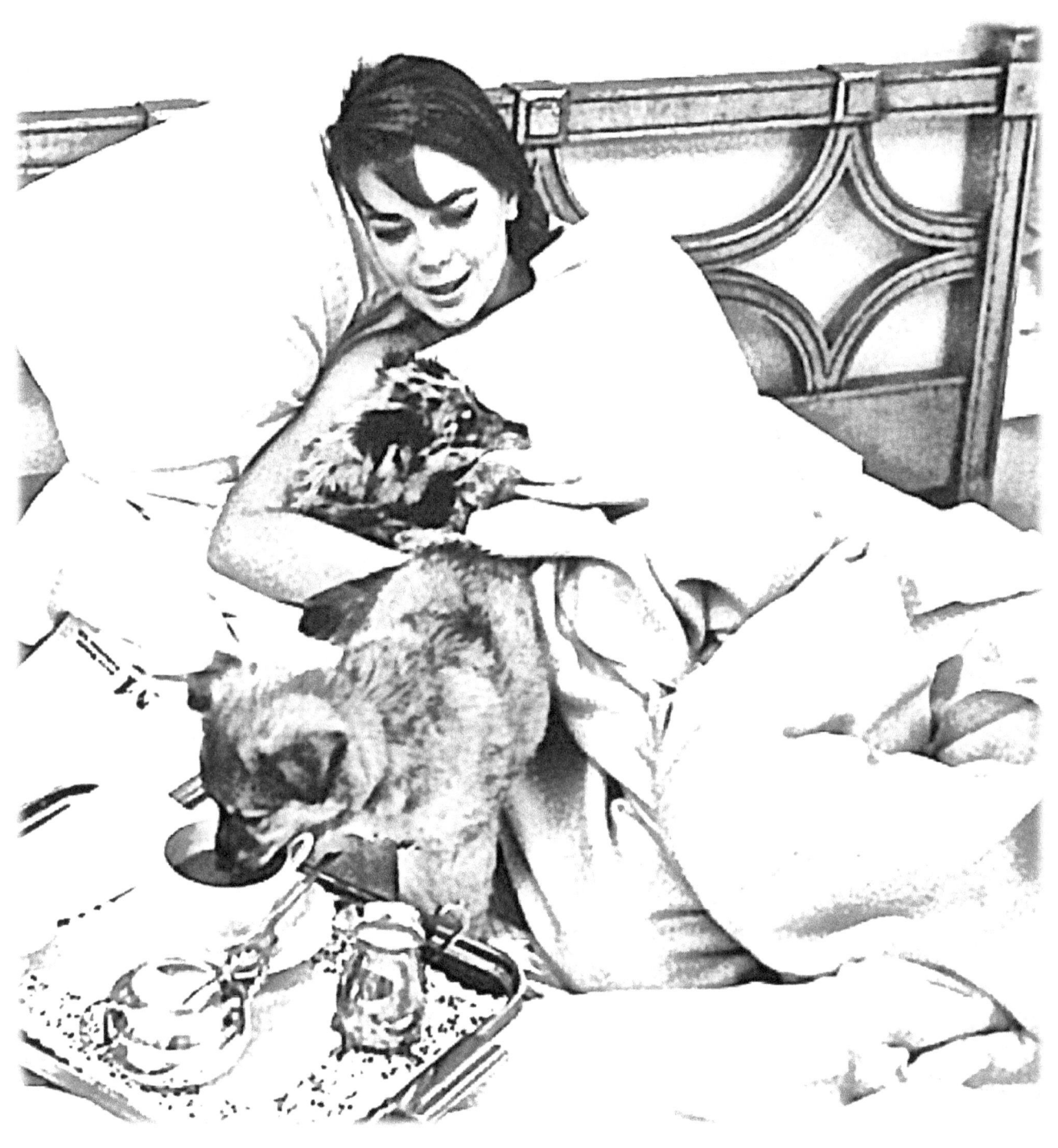

NATALIE WOOD

NATALIE WOOD 1938-1981
AMAZON AUTHOR PAGE: http://amzn.to/2g7qeAZ

ETSY SHOP, "JLA" :https://www.janetlongarts/shop/Etsy.com
ETSY VINTAGE SHOP: https://www.etsy.com/shop/AdoptionsLtd

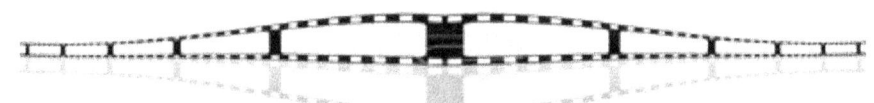

Your Notes & "test your medium" page.
Check your coloring tools to see how they work with this paper.